'Keenly researched and powerfully argued, this is a clarion call for the protection of children against insidious forms of harm. A courageous and hugely important book.'

– Jay Griffiths, author of Kith: The Riddle of the Childscape

'The nightmarish vision of this book is that parents have less and less ability to influence their children as the advertising and multimedia corporations colonise their minds. Children's bodies and brains are being steered towards future disease from junk food, they are desensitised to violence and prematurely sexualised, whilst their imaginations and empathy wither away from lack of creative play and interaction. It is a scary story and it left me genuinely wondering whether our current culture is itself abusing children.'

– Sue Gerhardt, psychotherapist and author of The Selfish Society

'When adults poison children, groom them for sex or expose them to extreme violence, we call it abuse. In this provocative and often shocking book, child protection expert Jim Wild rallies a wide range of expert evidence to show how "abuse" of this kind is rapidly becoming normalised across society – in the name of economic growth. As unregulated corporate greed threatens the physical and mental health of an entire generation, *Exploiting Childhood* is a book none of us can afford to ignore.'

– Sue Palmer, author of Toxic Childhood

'This vital book unpicks one of the tragedies of our time: the destruction of childhood by materialism, must-have selfishness and neoliberal ideology. From "make me a model parties" for six year old girls, complete with manicurists, hair dressers and a bespoke catwalk, to children watching 18,000 ads a year on their bedroom tellies, the picture to emerge is both grim and compelling. No wonder one child sex offender could so coldly observe "the culture did a lot of the grooming for me".

But this book also gives enormous hope. People – young and old – are resisting, rebelling and retelling their own stories. The chapter on critical thinking and the "hunt for assumptions" is beautifully pitched. We meet the inner city writing group Still Waters in a Storm which is an oasis that allows kids to regroup and rethink. And though we are reminded that the road to change is not easy, we also learn that we can have fun along the way – whether it is in the knowing lyrics of the rap scene or the wisdom of Shakespeare re-expressed in New York street argot.'

– Professor Gerard Hastings, Director of the Institute for Social Marketing and the Centre for Tobacco Control

Res   ty

'This well-evidenced and argued book exposes the pervasive and shocking forms of commercial exploitation and abuse of children by large corporations. Jim Wild and the expert chapter authors challenge us to face up to the misery and exploitation caused to parents, children and young people by these companies. The book makes a persuasive case for ensuring that children are protected from all forms of abuse, beyond those that our child protection systems currently recognise.'
– Brian Littlechild, Professor of Social Work, University of Hertfordshire, UK

'This important book recognises that child protection policy and practice has a very restricted view of what causes harm to children, and that we need to take seriously the growing evidence about the negative impact of commercial and corporate exploitation on children's well-being.'
– Nigel Parton, Professor of Applied Childhood Studies, University of Huddersfield

'Child protection is everyone's business – or at least it should be! This provocative book asks whether it is time to broaden the definition of "significant harm" because of the nature of the society we live in, the way we do business and the implications this has for our children. It focuses on many areas not traditionally seen as the core business of child protection professionals and challenges us to consider how our modern society impacts on children and their right to a safe childhood. Parents, professionals and politicians have a responsibility to understand the growing body of evidence concerning these risks. Agree or disagree, this book will challenge your thinking and urge you to question how some things in everyday life may be doing children more harm than good.'
– Trish O'Donnell, Development Manager, NSPCC

'This book should find a place on the reading lists of all safeguarding and children's services workers. It moves away from the usual focus on individual families and instead systematically examines the impact of society-wide commercial pressures on children.'
– Dr Terry Murphy, Teesside University and Social Work Action Network committee

'Over 12 years of delivering Local Safeguarding Children Board (LSCB) and single agency safeguarding training, I've found that attendees always want to know a safeguarding professional's opinions on the sorts of dilemmas and issues discussed in this book. This is an accessible, compelling and important book, and anyone involved in safeguarding children should read it and be aware of these issues.'
– Jane O'Daly, Trust Safeguarding Lead, Derby Hospitals NHS Foundation TrustExploiting Childhood

EXPLOITING CHILDHOOD

HOW FAST FOOD, MATERIAL OBSESSION AND PORN CULTURE ARE CREATING NEW FORMS OF CHILD ABUSE

EDITED BY JIM WILD

FOREWORDS BY CAMILA BATMANGHELIDJH
AND OLIVER JAMES

Jessica Kingsley *Publishers*
London and Philadelphia

First published in 2013
by Jessica Kingsley Publishers
73 Collier Street
London N1 9BE, UK
and
400 Market Street, Suite 400
Philadelphia, PA 19106, USA

www.jkp.com

Library of Congress Cataloging in Publication Data
Exploiting childhood : how fast food, material obsession and porn culture are
creating new forms of
child abuse / edited by Jim Wild ; forewords by Camila Batmanghelidjh and Oliver
James.
pages cm
ISBN 978-1-84905-368-6
1. Child welfare. 2. Child abuse. 3. Children--Social conditions--21st century. I.
Wild, Jim, 1953-
HV713.E89 2014
362.76--dc23
2013026939

British Library Cataloguing in Publication Data
A CIP catalogue record for this book is available from the British Library

ISBN 978 1 84905 368 6
eISBN 978 0 85700 742 1

Printed and bound in Great Britain by Bell & Bain Ltd., Glasgow

I would like to dedicate this book to a range of people, organisations and critical thinkers who have raised the spectre of new challenges in child protection.

CONTENTS

PART 2 **SEXUAL EXPLOITATION**

PART 3 **FIGHTING BACK AGAINST COMMERCIAL AND SEXUAL EXPLOITATION**

FOREWORD

CAMILA BATMANGHELIDJH

You have to wonder why in one of the most advanced countries in the world children continue to be violated at an epidemic rate. Millions are physically abused, neglected, sexually abused and emotionally traumatised. With the advancement of neuroscience and the sophistication of brain scanning, the chronic maltreatment vulnerable children endure shows up as functional and structural deficits in their brains. Child abuse is a lifelong challenge. When trauma has overpowered the child the best a child can hope for is that one day they will acquire some mastery over it. Flashbacks, dis-regulated emotional states, changes in immune system and cognitive impairments can be triggered by childhood maltreatment.

Not so visible is the chronic and insidious exposure of children to the rotten behaviour of adults. Neuropsychiatric research carried out at University of Cambridge demonstrates that significant damage to children's development can be perpetuated by constant low-level bickering, arguing, ignoring and negating within the family home. So whilst the dramatic assaults and their impact is now well understood, the perverted, almost normalised, harm children are exposed to, accumulatively becomes as toxic as the violent assaults.

The commercialisation of childhood, with children often being perceived as desirable little adults or as children used for sexual gratification, is adding to the mix of challenges a child in Britain has to negotiate. It really doesn't have to be this way. We don't have to harm our kids. They deserve better.

Society is, on the whole, very good at identifying the obvious perpetrators of abuse. We have systems to bring them to justice and to hold them accountable for the harm they do. But the conversation we're not having is how much children's sense of safety and their dignity is been assaulted through seemingly civil structures. The computer in our households traffic horrific images of violated children and some people switch on to be gratified. Milder versions of this appear in billposters, on our roads and in our magazines, disguised in adverts for clothing or drinks. It's adults who generate these images, who sell their products through the sexualisation of children. Our political leaders do little to prevent the harm done. Because children don't vote, they can't hold them accountable. They don't control the media so they're voiceless in a nation where adults, who are supposed to speak on their behalf, don't do so because they don't think of the world from a vulnerable child's perspective.

I hope in reading this book we will have reflected back at us the wrongs we have so delusionary normalised. We have to have faith in the humanity we share in common and I can only hope that, in reading this amazing book, we'll have the courage to stop abuse when we come across it.

Camila Batmanghelidjh
Psychotherapist, and founder of
The Place2Be and Kids Company London, UK

FOREWORD

OLIVER JAMES

Jim Wild will outline in his introduction that the chapters in this book will require that we broaden our concept of the fundamental causes of harm in young people. Whilst physical and sexual abuse, emotional neglect and other forms of maltreatment will always be a major concern, we have to accept that the wider cultural and economic environment is also contributing to the horrifying levels of distress that surveys consistently find. The key factor has been political economics.

From 1979 in Britain and from 1980 in America, Thatcherism and Reagonomics created a form of political economy, which I term 'Selfish Capitalism'. It directly caused a substantial rise in emotional problems through ramping up consumerism, unrealistic material expectations and massive personal debts.

Selfish Capitalism has four defining features. The first is that the success of a company is judged largely by its current share price, rather than by its underlying strength or its contribution to the society or economy.

The second is a strong drive to privatise collective goods, such as water, gas and electric utilities.

The third is minimal regulation of financial services and labour markets, including the introduction of working practices that strongly favour employers and disfavour trade unions, making it easier to hire and fire. Alongside this, taxes are not concerned with the redistribution of wealth, making it easier for corporations and the rich to avoid them, and to use tax havens within the law. There is also a substantial increase in household debt because lenders are permitted to advertise heavily to populations, leading to widespread use of credit cards, loans and mortgages. Debt becomes a natural state – nationally and individually.

The fourth defining feature is the conviction that consumption and market forces can meet human needs of almost every kind.

Given these characteristics, it is not surprising that Selfish Capitalist societies create citizens who tend to be more materialistic than ones in relatively unselfish capitalist societies, like those in mainland Western Europe. Materialism is placing too high a value on money, possessions, appearances and fame. For 50 years, the per capita spend on advertising in America has been four times that in mainland Europe. Twice as much has been spent in the UK. Advertising is designed deliberately to conflate confected wants with real needs.

Materialistic people are significantly more likely to suffer the commonest emotional problems – depression, neuroses, personality disorders, substance abuse and eating disorders (James 2007). It follows that if you increase the materialism of a population, you would expect a rise in emotional problems.

In my book *The Selfish Capitalist* I present evidence from the World Health Organization's 15-nation survey of mental illness that there is twice as much mental illness in the materialistic English-speaking nations compared with mainland Europe. I also cite strong evidence that the amount of mental illness among young people doubled between 1980 and 2007 in the UK.

Young women were particularly harmed, and in some respects, their suffering has been that of the canaries in the 'Selfish Capitalist cage'. A British study of a large sample of 15-year-olds showed that the prevalence of emotional problems from the top two social classes rose from 24 per cent in 1987 to 38 per cent in 1999. This rise had continued when the survey was repeated in 2006, the proportion rising to 43 per cent.

The concerns the young women gave for their distress were their body images, day-to-day school pressures, exams and family problems. The body image distress is particularly pertinent. Since the 1970s there have been studies proving that if young women are exposed to images of exceptionally good-looking and slim other females, they feel worse afterwards. When their male partners are so exposed, not only are they less satisfied with their current partner, they actually record feeling less love for them. In the largely unregulated contemporary cultures found in America and the UK, females are exposed to huge numbers of such images daily. It is hardly surprising if they subsequently report discontent about their bodies.

Put crudely, we have been turned into a population of 'Shop Till You Drop', 'It Could Be You', credit-fuelled consumer junkies. This book demands that you take this into account when listening to children report their anxieties and feelings of depression. It is also a wake-up call in terms of the kind of society we have built and the one that we should be aiming for.

Oliver James
Psychologist, journalist and author, London, UK

REFERENCE

James, O. (2007) *Affluenza*. London: Vermilion.

ACKNOWLEDGEMENTS

First, I would like to thank those who I love dearly and sometimes let down because of my constant activism: my partner Joan Healey, daughters Emma, Chloe and Bridie, and granddaughters Evie and Emily.

My friends for over 20 years, John Casson and Lynne Jones have always been available when I needed support through good and bad times.

Those at Jessica Kingsley Publishers, in particular, Stephen Jones the Commissioning Editor who had several well-mannered duels with me over the book's title and has always been faithful to the project, and Allison Walker the Production Editor who has always been so hard working and available.

I want to acknowledge people and organisations that have helped me run the events and encourage the publication. Some simply gave me work when I have found myself having to leave places of employment because I could not accept the lack of ethics or blew the whistle on bad practice. Others gave me time, support or encouragement and have influenced or inspired me into action. They include: David Footie, Sharon Girling, Matt Kenyon, Michael Kerman, Graham Whitehead, Mark Sobey (for doing the right thing), Susie Orbach, Oliver James, Jo Neale, Julie Bindel, The British Association of Social Workers, Peter Beresford, Glenis Hurst-Robson, Damien Simpson, John Goodwin, BASPCAN, Still Waters in the Storm, Carol Holt, Susan Wordsworth, Cindy Campbell and Glen Dickson. Particular thanks to Professor Chris Goddard and Professor Brian Littlechild who have encouraged me and evaluated my projects in their own time. Liz Kelly and Maddy Coy have always been willing to support me and are such incredibly committed academics. I would especially like to thank everyone at Kids Company for helping with practical resources when the events leading to this book took place, and their inspirational leader Camila Batmanghelidjh who has always given empowering words of support. I would also like to acknowledge the amazing Professor Gail Dines who is ahead of us all with her unique style of teaching, ceaseless campaigning and concern about the effects of pornography.

CHAPTER 1

INTRODUCTION

JIM WILD

This book has been written to describe the emerging problems and dilemmas associated with the widespread and insidious exploitation of children today, across all sections of society. You may find some of the material shocking, perhaps provocative in places, but its overall aim is to make you think, and question your own assumptions about our collective responsibility for the welfare of children in society today.

My own background is as a child protection trainer, consultant and activist, having worked in the field of social work and child protection for many years. In 2012 I organised a series of events in London for child protection workers, which featured a range of international speakers, designed to contribute new and original perspectives on widespread harm being inflicted on children arising from commercial activity, whether it be sexualised marketing and publicity or aggressive marketing of junk foods.

What was striking about these events was that many professionals who attended were profoundly moved and shocked by much of what they heard, but their common response was, 'But what can we do?' The intention of this book is to explore some of the issues first raised in the series of events, and to think upon the question – what can and should we be doing to address these harmful influences, and are these encroachments into the lives of children and young people creating new forms of harm?

It should be pointed out that many of the speakers and contributors in this publication do not have a background in child protection and do not speak in a unified voice. Not all would agree that the concerns described within this book should be considered as new forms of abuse, and the diversity represented within the book is also reflected in the different styles of writing – some dwelling on research findings and statistics, others offering a more personally informed perspective. What all featured contributors do share is high levels of expertise in their own particular areas of interest, and all contribute vital evidence for the reader to consider when reflecting on how we should be responding.

COMMERCIAL AND CORPORATE EXPLOITATION

Children and young people live in a world where big corporations and commercial interests employ some of the most talented and creative individuals in their marketing and advertising companies to devise astounding ways of influencing parents, children and young people to part with money.

A wide range of techniques and psychological manipulations are used by corporate and commercial interests to get children and young people 'onside' – they are encouraged to eat, dress, purchase or develop 'aspirational lifestyles' for a wide range of consumer products or behave or act in ways that seem demonstrative of the latest fashion or trend (Mayo and Nairn 2009).

In the UK the average child now watches around 17 hours of TV a week, three out of four children between the ages of 5 and 16 have a TV in their bedroom and they watch on average 18,000 adverts each year (Beder, Varney and Gosden 2009). Recent mobile phone technology provides a greater opportunity for 'personalisation' and for corporate interests to form significant 'relationships' with children and young people. It is a process built on a cycle of desire, acquisition and dissatisfaction (Salecl 2011) as new and more exciting and exclusive technology is produced, resulting in anxiety, uncertainty and the need to uphold and exhibit the notion of ourselves through a public display of consumer affluence.

In the book *This Little Kiddy Went to Market*, Beder, Varney and Gosden (2009) suggest that many businesses set out to deceive. Sharon Beder claims this takes the form of:

- the use of celebrities to exploit a child's trust in authority figures

- focusing on gifts and giveaways rather than the actual product that is being sold

- the use of jargon and culturally complex language to take advantage of a child's limited vocabulary

- the excessive use of emotional triggers to exploit a child's insecurities and gullibility.

Countries differ in their legislative action, but for the most part global markets are relatively free in allowing the commercial targeting of children and young people and there is little ability to distinguish between a child of eight, a teenager and a mature adult. Some Scandinavian countries have managed to limit commercial targeting on TV, but in reality there are high levels of freedom to target anyone with the wide range of electronic devices that children and adults now use (Beder *et al.* 2009).

In recent times, the UK Government has responded to growing concern expressed by parents' and children's organisations relating to the sexual and commercial pressures on children. It commissioned Reg Bailey, Chief Executive of Mothers' Union, to carry out an independent review entitled *Letting Children Be Children*, which was published in June 2011. This could be seen as a watershed moment.

The report made a range of recommendations including:

- providing parents with one single website to make it easier to complain about any programme, advert, product or service

- putting age restrictions on music videos to prevent children buying sexually explicit videos and to guide broadcasters over when to show them

- covering up sexualised images on the front pages of magazines and newspapers so they are not in easy sight of children

- making it easier for parents to block adult and age-restricted material from the internet by giving every customer a choice at the point of purchase over whether they want adult content on their home internet, laptops or smart phones

- retailers offering age-appropriate clothes for children – the retail industry should sign up to the British Retail Consortium's new guidelines, which check and challenge the design, buying, display and marketing of clothes, products and services for children

- restricting outdoor adverts containing sexualised imagery where large numbers of children are likely to see them, for example, near schools, nurseries and playgrounds

- giving greater weight to the views of parents in the regulation of pre-watershed TV, rather than viewers as a whole, about what is suitable for children to watch

- banning the employment of children under 16 as brand ambassadors and in peer-to-peer marketing, and improving parents' awareness of advertising and marketing techniques aimed at children.

However, the report was seen by some as a disappointment on a number of levels. First, Bailey himself was in no way an expert in the areas he explored in the report and, while the report was independent and commissioned by the Department for Education, some questioned the appropriateness of the review being authored by an individual with links to a faith-based organisation (though it's worth adding that Mother's Union distanced itself from involvement with the review). Second, at times his conclusions seemed naive about such terms as 'the watershed' on TV, only allowing more adult content to screen after 9pm, given many children have access to mobile phones, laptop computers and TV in the privacy of their own rooms. Indeed, many children and young people are more competent and able than their parents when working with new technology, and companies providing access to online facilities are anxious about the implications of restricting their customers' right to choose.

It would also seem unlikely that with economic problems, double-dip recessions and austerity, politicians would be interested in restricting commercial and corporation advertising, which could add yet another obstacle to growth in the economy.

So in many ways the Bailey report has been seen by many as a token gesture to the concerns and debates about the issues discussed in this book and is unlikely to have an impact as new technologies move rapidly on, allowing corporate, commercial and sexual exploitation in a relentless pursuit of children and young people.

The view that children and young people are captive to consumerism is not a new concept although what is new, and what this book aims to explore, is to suggest that commercial exploitation should be considered a cause of 'significant harm' to the child – a specialist term within child protection that distinguishes an action to be so harmful as to constitute a form of abuse.

Below, I explain some of the basic terms and functions that relate to child protection for those readers who are not already familiar with them.

CHILD ABUSE

The definition of child abuse has developed and changed over several decades as resources, training, research and testimonies of survivors develop our understanding of what happens to children and young people. Within the UK the definition can be seen as any form of activity that can cause a child 'significant harm', which is further clarified by four separate sub-categories – emotional abuse, physical abuse, sexual abuse and neglect. Government guidance must be followed by statutory and voluntary bodies. The latest Government guidance for Local Safeguarding Children Boards is in the publication *Working Together to Safeguard Children*, which states that the safeguarding and promoting the welfare of children is defined as:

- protecting children from maltreatment

- preventing impairment of children's health or development

- ensuring that children grow up in circumstances consistent with the provision of safe and effective care

- taking action to enable all children to have the best outcomes.

(HM Government 2013, p.7)

The Government has defined 'significant harm' as follows:

There are no absolute criteria on which to rely when judging what constitutes significant harm. Consideration of the severity of ill-treatment may include the degree and the extent of physical harm, the duration and frequency of abuse and neglect, the extent of premeditation, and the presence or degree of threat, coercion, sadism and bizarre or unusual elements. Each of these elements has been associated with more severe effects on the child, and/or relatively greater difficulty in helping the child overcome the adverse impact of the maltreatment. Sometimes, a single traumatic event may constitute significant harm, for example, a violent assault, suffocation or poisoning. More often, significant harm is a compilation of significant events, both acute and long-standing, which interrupt, change or damage the child's physical and psychological development. (HM Government 2013, p.8)

When there are concerns that a child may be suffering significant harm, professionals have a duty to follow procedures. This can result in an investigation from social workers and the police to find out if a child is suffering, or is likely to suffer, significant harm (Children Act 1989). Court proceedings or emergency protection orders could be taken if a child is deemed at risk of significant harm.

Every local authority has a Local Safeguarding Children Board (LSCB), which is responsible for local arrangements for protecting children and young people. They provide inter-agency guidelines for child protection and have a duty to audit or regulate the effectiveness of child protection services.

Concerns about corporate and commercial exploitation of children and young people are not on the agenda of LSCB and have received little attention to date. Indeed, the suggestion that we should widen the definition of significant harm is unlikely to be warmly greeted by services, which are already stretched at present levels of resourcing.

However, limited resources are no reason to abandon these questions, which must be scrutinised and explored. I am not so naive to suggest we categorise vast numbers of children and young people as being 'abused' compared to traditional notions of child abuse: this would be insulting and completely unacceptable. I am, however, suggesting we may need to take another look at how we define 'significant harm' and widen this definition accordingly.

COMPARABLE EXAMPLES OF SIGNIFICANT HARM

There is a legal duty to intervene if a child is deemed to be suffering significant harm and below are a range of hypothetical case examples, with which I attempt to compare and contrast the issues between child abuse within the family and similar concerns but within the context of commercial and corporate exploitation of children and young people.

Clearly, we live in a world where commercialism and advertising is a part of what we absorb day to day, and we have services that are stretched and under resourced. Yet these examples raise critical debates important to child protection and wider resource provision.

As the reader explores the examples, they may find the following questions (taken from a variety of child protection texts and modified to explore commercialism; see Brown, Moore and Turvey 2009; Calder 2009; Horwath 2009) useful to consider.

- What is the nature of the commercial or corporate targeting and in what context are we exploring these concerns?

- Is there an impact on the child's health and development and is there any objective evidence that corporate and commercial targeting have adverse effects on children and young people?

- What is its significance – the extent of the impact on the child or young person in the short, medium and long term?

- What are the psychological effects – on well-being, self-esteem and identity?

- What is the level of targeting – its extent, duration and frequency?

- What ability do children and young people have to give objective consent and informed knowledge when they are targeted?

This final question is particularly complex as many corporations employ services of companies that claim to be able to assist consumers in making choices at unconscious or subliminal levels (Monbiot 2011).

EXAMPLE 1: FOOD

Example 1a: Parental poisoning of a child

Anonymous but credible information has been given to statutory services that a parent is intentionally mixing a substance in their child's food that will make that child ill. It is understood the parent knows that their action is likely to affect that child's short- and long-term health in a negative way. The child has no knowledge the parent is administering this substance in their food. The parent does not administer it every day; indeed, several days may go by and the child is free of any poison administered by their parent. On other occasions, the parent significantly increases the substance, which can sometimes result in the child becoming ill and unable to attend school.

Example 1b: A corporate food manufacturer

A food corporation produces a new processed food product targeting children and young people. It focuses on the cheaper end of the market and any child or young person can purchase the products freely. The product has ingredients high in sugar, salt and saturated fats. The targeting involves a range of techniques and the products aim at breakfast, lunch and afternoon 'snacks'. They have calculated the average amount of money children and young people have each day and price these products within this total. However, if eaten daily by children and young people there will be a negative effect on their short- and long-term health outcomes. The company markets these products rigorously through some of the most creative advertising consultants available, suggesting these are 'fun' food products. They run the ads through web-based strategies and young people's magazines and have a website where young people can register an individual number from the product and enter a 'draw' to obtain free tickets to music festivals or get free downloads. The company also obtains the services of celebrities and occasionally links the food product they sell to new films providing a free gift and the allure of possible prizes. The company knows families are busy and need 'food' that is quick, and particular branding and artwork provides the allure of marketing the product to give strength and energy. There are no health warnings on the product concerned and it is one of the most popular brands amongst 7–12-year-olds. The product is sold to millions of children and young people in the UK and around the world.

In Example 1a there is a need for statutory intervention, which will include Section 47 investigations (UK statutory investigations to ascertain whether a child is suffering abuse, where, should concerns be validated, a case can be made to remove the child). There may be a need for the parent to undergo a forensic assessment and a protracted court case could ensue.

In Example 1b there are no major concerns about the food manufacturer's activities in terms of child protection. They are free to advertise wherever they choose, to millions of children and young people, and will employ a range of strategies and tactics to obtain loyalty to their products and brand.

If a parent is knowingly poisoning their own child to the extent that it may produce a negative health outcome sometime in the future, statutory child protection systems would need to act because this is categorised as child abuse. By comparison, to what extent are corporations held to account when intensively selling knowingly harmful foods to children and young people, particularly if eating their food product/s on a regular basis will result in problems such as obesity, diabetes, high blood pressure and emerging heart disease? As important, at a time when children and young people are impressionable, the standard is set for future eating habits that will be difficult to alter.

In the UK there are major concerns about the health of children and young people:

- Ninety-two per cent of children consume more saturated fat than is recommended.

- Eighty-six per cent are consuming too much salt and sugar.

- Twenty-seven per cent of 15-year-olds get drunk regularly.

- Ninety-six per cent of children and young people do not eat enough fruit and vegetables.

- There have been warnings of health complexities in the future from health campaigners and the British Medical Association.

(Beder, Varney and Gosden 2009)

Are both examples so different? The first is discreet, episodic and dangerous to a single child and undertaken by a parent who clearly has major psychological problems. The second is undertaken within a climate where millions of children and young people will be influenced within a vast global market. Children and young people who habitually eat these products daily will suffer devastating health problems, yet this is not seen as abusive. Why is this the case?

EXAMPLE 2: WOMEN AND BODIES

Example 2a: Parents' concerning behaviour relating to their daughter's appearance

Parents of a 13-year-old girl are anxious their daughter is becoming overweight, although she is well within the parameters of the 'normal' range for her age. However, both parents constantly call her derogatory names and suggest she should stop eating as much or she will never get a boyfriend. They have restricted her intake of food and at times only allow her water. The mother is concerned about a 'blemish' on her daughter's face and wants her to take time off school to seek a consultation with a cosmetic surgeon. The school staff have increasingly become concerned about this young person who seems to be developing early signs of an eating disorder and was found after lunch on several occasions being sick in the toilet. The young person is tearful and upset and recently disclosed to a teacher she thought she was ugly and wanted to die. It has also been discovered that the mother has recently undertaken a course in the administering of Botox and her 13-year-old daughter has experienced several injections to her face. The parent has told her daughter it will enhance her beauty.

> ### Example 2b: Corporate and commercial targeting of girls and young women
>
> A new fashion and lifestyle magazine for young women is about to be launched with major celebrities actively involved in its promotion. Many of the stories and reports cover a range of fears teenage girls seem 'preoccupied' with – weight, image, clothes, relationships and celebrity information. Models in the magazine are size zero and there are interviews with stars who have had cosmetic surgery. Many of the features are linked to programmes on TV that explore beauty fears, making people younger, and individual self-esteem issues where people have had their lives 'transformed' through 'cosmetic' re-corrective surgery. There are also competitions that require young women to provide email addresses, which can be sold on to commercial interests who can then target them via mobile phones and email.

Exploitation of women's bodies according to Orbach is orchestrated by 'legitimate' businesses:

- Bodies (particularly women's) are becoming a site of serious suffering and disorder (programmes linked to teen and celebrity magazines) to the point that most young people know intimate details of celebrities...now 88 per cent of young women (12–16) feel anxious or unhappy with how they look.

- Cosmetic industry is worth over £14 billion.

- A relentless desire to reshape the body (predicated by loan companies and the cosmetic industry and linked to cosmetic 'qualifications') has taken place over the past ten years.

- Cosmetic surgical procedures are occupying more space on TV adverts (growth rate of one billion a year).

(Orbach 2009)

In Example 2a there are clearly concerns that both parents are causing this young person emotional distress by their actions. Statutory services would need to make enquiries about this young person's welfare and the parents' obsessive concerns. However, commercial and corporate companies are able to constantly project unrealistic images of what young women should look like and suggest that certain products can lead to more desirable outcomes. Yet while the corporate and commercial world continue to bombard girls and young women with products they claim will transform their lives, they have the potential to cause distress, anxiety and the obsessive need to diet.

EXAMPLE 3: VIOLENCE AND PORNOGRAPHY

Example 3a: A father teaching his son violence and abuse

A father who is known to be involved in criminal activities and has served prison sentences for violence towards other people, teaches his 12-year-old son 'how to look after himself'. He has shown him ways of inflicting harm through close physical contact, how to 'use' a knife and has recently taken him to an isolated area to shoot handguns. The son also watches pornography with his father, in particular films where men humiliate women and are aggressive during sexual contact. The father has purchased a 'commando' style knife for his son. The son recently had a fight at school where his opponent was cut with the 'commando' knife, was hospitalised and required stitches. An urgent planning meeting of professionals has been called to discuss the possibility of statutory intervention. Professionals are concerned that the father is implicated in the promotion of violent behaviour that is dangerous and potentially lethal. Agencies are also anxious about the derogatory way the son treats female peers as he was recently suspended for making inappropriate sexual suggestions to girls in his class.

> ### Example 3b: The corporate and commercial legitimising of violent activities for boys
>
> A computer games manufacturer is devising the newest and most graphic game yet in this sector. It is aware that there will be restrictions on selling this game to younger people, but knows that it can use product placement techniques at supermarkets to assist in selling the product and is aware of 'pester power' techniques that enable children and young people to obtain compliance from parents to 'just give in'. The company is also aware that many boys will have access to credit cards and can devise other ways of purchasing these games. The violence will be the most graphic ever produced and the player will be directed by a leader of mercenaries who is the most heroic, saving the player from death on several occasions. The game leads to a final enactment where the 'leader' is about to be attacked from behind and because the player is out of ammunition, the only way to save him is to use a knife to cut the throat of the enemy. The player gets points for the level of strength used to kill the adversary and to kill him the player must be unequivocal and the scene will be bloody. But the player will be the winner – if you are not immediate in your actions you lose. The game ends with the player as the hero.

According to Connell (2001) there is now a clear connection between men and initiation into 'violence', and a wide range of ways that the corporate and commercial world make products and games that replicate and glorify violent behaviour. There is also a wide range of computer games that boys have access to that are vivid and realistic in war and combat. One of the latest is *Call of Duty: Modern Warfare*; the violence is excessive and realistic – men are killed in grotesque and realistic ways and the player of the game is encouraged to replicate vivid violent actions without any explanation or context. There is also evidence that boys as young as eight have been watching pornography on the internet. According to Dines (2010), 'the power that men have over women in porn sex is encoded into the sex acts and the physical and verbal abuse that accompanies them'.

In Example 3a there are criminal concerns about the way a father is helping his child to use a knife and gun and also major concerns in the father accessing pornography and watching this with his son. It would seem that both the police and child protection staff would need to take immediate action to investigate what the father has being 'teaching' his son and criminal prosecutions may follow.

In Example 3b large corporations can produce extreme violence in computer games and through their market research specifically target boys and young men. The internet is also a vast and open market for children and young people to access pornography. Whilst there is parental control software to restrict child viewing, many young people are more competent than their parents with computer technology and are able to access ways of turning this software off. However, the amelioration and acceptance of graphic, violent and relentless violence is seen as commercially acceptable business.

Again, I pose the question: how different are these examples?

IS CORPORATE, COMMERCIAL AND SEXUAL EXPLOITATION A FORM OF CHILD ABUSE?

In many ways this book is an attempt to raise the debate about issues and concerns across a specific range of contexts.

Tim Lobstein explores junk food and a range of critical issues that clearly show the link between obesity and poor-quality food products specifically aimed at children and young people and the likelihood of bad health outcomes.

Gail Dines considers the effects of pornography and how we can presently only speculate the effects of hypersexualised sexual imagery on emerging young adults and their understanding of gender relations.

To Renata Salecl, these issues raise more fundamental philosophical questions relating to the cultivation of endless consumer choice, which, rather than being a positive development, has seen children and adults become engulfed by anxiety and uncertainty.

The juxtaposition of endless choice is how children and young people manage where families live in acute poverty and children and young people face constant ridicule from peers for having old or dated merchandise; Agnes Nairn's contribution highlights the tensions, problems and complexities of growing up poor and not 'fitting in'.

This gives you a taste of some of what follows. I hope that you find this book thought provoking and stimulating and, as you read about some of the deeply concerning and widespread activities being carried out by companies today, do keep in mind some of the comparisons I have made in this introductory chapter about the distinction between significant harm and commercial activity.

REFERENCES

Beder, S., Varney, W. and Gosden, R. (2009) *This Little Kiddy Went to Market: The Corporate Capture of Childhood*. London: Pluto Press.

Brown, L., Moore, S. and Turvey, D. (2009) *Analysis and Critical Thinking in Assessment: Change Project Pilot Resources*. Dartington: Research into Practice.

Calder, M. (ed.) (2009) *Sexual Abuse Assessments*. Lyme Regis: Russell House Publishing.

Connell, R. (2001) *On Men and Violence*. Sydney: University of Sydney.

Dines, G. (2010) *Pornland*. Boston, MA: Beacon Press.

HM Government (2013) *Working Together to Safeguard Children*. London: Department for Education, HM Government.

Horwath, J. (ed.) (2009) *The Child's World: The Comprehensive Guide to Assessing Children in Need* (2nd edition). London: Jessica Kingsley Publishers.

Mayo, E. and Nairn, A. (2009) *Consumer Kids: How Big Business is Grooming Our Children for Profit*. London: Constable & Robinson.

Monbiot, G. (2011) 'Advertising is a poison that demeans even love – and we're hooked on it.' *The Guardian*, Monday 24 October 2011. Available at www.guardian.co.uk/commentisfree/2011/oct/24/advertising-poison-hooked, accessed on 16 May 2013.

Orbach, S. (2009) *Bodies*. London: Profile Books.

Salecl, R. (2011) *The Tyranny of Choice*. London: Profile Books.

Warburton, W. and Braunstein, D. (2012) *Growing Up Fast and Furious*. Sydney: The Federation Press.

PART 1

COMMERCIAL EXPLOITATION

CHAPTER 2

ARGUMENTS, BULLIES AND FEELING POOR

HOW CONSUMER CULTURE AFFECTS CHILDREN'S RELATIONSHIPS

PROFESSOR AGNES NAIRN

The global children's market is estimated to be worth almost US$2 trillion – roughly the size of India's GDP (Lindstrom and Seybold 2003). In the UK alone we spend an average of almost £220,000 on a single child from birth to age 21 and this figure has risen by 50 per cent in just three years (Liverpool Victoria Friendly Society 2012; Smithers 2012). It is clear that bringing up children is increasingly about buying 'stuff'. This development has a number of implications for children's well-being and this chapter looks in particular at how marketing to children affects their relationships with the most important people in their lives: their family and their friends. It also shows how the stark income inequality in the UK exacerbates the negative effects of commercialism on children's happiness.

The chapter is organised in five sections. The first looks at the growing number of areas of children's lives that are now influenced by commercial imperatives. The second reviews the research that shows how consumer culture is associated with family conflict, something that has particularly negative outcomes for children. The third looks at how heavily advertised desirable brands can affect peer relationships and are strongly associated with bullying. The fourth examines how those who are most economically disenfranchised are most vulnerable to the negative effects of consumer culture. And the final section makes some suggestions for how those working with children and young people can help them navigate the commercial world.

THE COMMERCIALISATION OF JUST ABOUT EVERYTHING

Children now spend twice as much time in front of a screen (TV, computer, games console, mobile phone, iPod, iPad tablet, etc.) as they do in a classroom, and they spend 150 per cent more time in front of a screen than with their parents (Mayo and Nairn 2009). With the exception of the BBC, the TV children watch is funded by advertising and the 'free' content on the internet is funded either by selling finely targeted advertising slots or selling information about children's internet behaviour to third parties so that they, in turn, can market to them. Video games are sponsored by brands that place subtle commercial messages within the action scenes, and advertising on mobile phones is on the increase. So it is clear that an enormous amount of children's time is spent in the company of people trying to sell them stuff.

Increasingly, children's play is also becoming commercialised. Between a quarter and a third of all toys are licensed, which means that a big part of their appeal to children is simply their association with a heavily advertised and promoted film or TV show such as *Star Wars*, *Spider-Man* or *Toy Story*. At the time of writing, Amazon has no fewer than 26,649 Spider-Man items for sale.[1] What this means for children and their parents is that they have to pay more for their toys – licensed toys cost an average of 57 per cent more than unlicensed toys (NPD Group 2012). We pay over half as much again for pyjamas that have Dora the Explorer on them rather than simple stripes, spots or flowers.

The ultimate push behind this licensing trend is, of course, not creating more inspiring, exciting toys that meet the needs of parents or children but making more cash for shareholders of the massive corporations that own these licenses, the biggest of

---

1   www.amazon.co.uk/s/ref=nb_sb_noss_1?url=search-alias%3Daps&field-keywords=spiderman, accessed on 22 October 2012.

which is undoubtedly the Disney corporation. One of their most successful 'properties' is *High School Musical*, which has made close to US$1 billion in merchandising, a figure that dwarfs the production cost of the original film, a mere US$4.2 million. In 2012 the 'Mouse House' added the Star Wars franchise to its stable of original characters such as Mickey and Donald; Pixar favourites including Buzz Lightyear and Nemo; and Marvel Comic heroes like Spider-Man. They paid €4.05 billion to buy Lucasfilm, a deal that was concluded less for the potential to make good films and more for the cash-generating capability of the licensing, most of which is for children's toys (Block 2012). One Wall Street investor who was encouraging his clients to invest in Disney at the height of the *High School Musical* frenzy stated that, 'The great thing about having a hit like this [*High School Musical*] is that there are many different ways of monetizing that hit over and over' (Mayo and Nairn 2009, p.156). It is not, therefore, the welfare of children at the heart of licensed toy marketing but a 'monetizing' machine.

The commercial world has intervened in children's outdoor play too. A recent Playday survey (2008) asked children where they experienced adventurous play. For almost half of those interviewed adventurous play was associated not with building tree houses or dams but in the closely supervised and controlled environment of a theme park. Fewer than a third now associate adventure with outdoor natural space. This provides a stark contrast with what their own parents said about their childhoods: only 16 per cent experienced adventurous play in theme parks whilst 70 per cent had done so in outdoor natural space. The economic consequences of this dramatic shift in play habits within just one generation are great. It costs an average family several hundred pounds to have a day out to a theme park (even before the inevitable gift shop visit) whilst a trip to the forest or a common is free. Again, shareholder returns are paramount and again, Disney is at the forefront. In 2012 Disney's profits from theme parks increased by 10 per cent to US$3.2 billion contributing to a 30 per cent increase in the corporation's overall profits (US$1.8 billion net profit on US$11 billion turnover) (Barnes 2012), making it just about the best current investment on the US stock market.

Of course, no one is forcing us to go to theme parks or to buy licensed merchandise, but imperceptibly we seem to have bought into the idea (literally) that if we are not paying for something for our children then it is not really good enough for them. If we part with cash then somehow we must be better parents. A recent example of this is the emergence of the 'edutainment' market, which encourages parents to pay for DVDs such as 'Baby Einstein' or 'Baby Mozart', with the promise that plugging their child into these expensive programmes will somehow turn them into brilliant mathematicians or musicians. An extreme case of this broke out in China this summer with parents paying almost £10,000 for a summer course in Shanghai in the belief that their children would learn to read a book in just 20 seconds (Branigan 2012). This is an extraordinary example but a review commissioned by the UK Government into the sexualisation and commercialisation of childhood revealed just how pervasive the commercialisation of parenthood has become (Bailey 2011). As parents said to the review team:

- 'I feel pressure from other parents – that parent's done it, why haven't I and should I?'

- 'The problem is that parents sometimes feel the peer pressure too and often feel almost forced to buy certain products because other parents are. They feel like bad parents if they don't.'

We can see therefore that the children's market is massive, growing fast and fuelled by a handful of giant corporations answerable to their investors. As shareholders need growth from their investments, the monetising machine has to keep selling parents more and more. Parents in turn are feeling the pressure. But what effect does this have on children's well-being? It is to this that I turn in the next section.

CONSUMER CULTURE AND FAMILY CONFLICT

In recent research by UNICEF UK on the well-being of children in the UK, Sweden and Spain, 8–14-year-olds were asked 'What makes a good day?' and 'What makes a bad day?' (Nairn *et al.* 2011). The most common response from children of all ages and backgrounds in the three countries was that a good day was one spent with friends and family whilst a bad day was one where there were fights and arguments with parents, siblings or friends. There is now a solid body of research that shows how consumer culture and advertising are closely linked in various complex but consistent ways with disruption, tension and arguments between children, their family and their peers. This section considers family conflict.

'Pester power' is exercised by children over their parents when they nag, whine and beg to be bought something until the exasperated parent relinquishes control over their better judgement and purchases the toys, sweets or whatever the child is demanding. The technique is particularly effective when exercised in a busy shop when the parent is tired! This obviously adds to the pressure contemporary UK parents are already under – as we saw above – and children are acutely aware of the power they hold. The Bailey review (introduced by Jim Wild on p.19) found that nearly a third of children say that they will always keep on and on asking for something they want until their parents give in (Bailey 2011). More than half said they sometimes do this, while a mere 15 per cent said they never pursue their pestering until their parents submit. This is obviously irritating and annoying for parents, but it goes deeper than that.

Pester power is strongly related to how much TV advertising a child sees: unsurprisingly the more TV advertising a child is exposed to the more they pester their parents for advertised products (Buijzen and Valkenburg 2003). What is worrying, however, is that the more children nag their parents in this way the less satisfied they are not just with their parents but with their lives in general (Buijzen and Valkenburg 2003). They are more discontented and less happy. It seems that children who nag their parents a lot are likely on average to be met with more refusals, which not only leads to immediate disappointment and annoyance with the parent but also becomes generalised so that life overall seems rather tainted. American sociology professor Juliet Schor (2004, p.55) puts it like this:

> It's important to recognise the nature of the corporate message: kids and products are aligned together in a really great, fun place, while parents, teachers, and other adults inhabit an oppressive, drab, and joyless world. The lesson to kids is that it's the product, not your parent who's really on your side.

Other research shows that these household negotiations, disagreements and tensions are strongly linked not only to low life satisfaction but to depression, anxiety, low self-esteem and a range of psychosomatic symptoms (Nairn, Ormrod and Bottomley 2007). Central to this dynamic is the way in which advertising nurtures materialistic values in children. We now know that children exposed to a lot of advertising tend to be more materialistic, which means that they focus their lives on getting the latest stuff, which they believe will make them happy, popular with their peers and even protect them from bullying – a baseless hope as it turns out because materialism in childhood and adulthood is strongly linked to a range of mental health problems (Schor 2004). The dynamics of the links between advertising, materialism, family disputes and unhappiness are of course extremely complex and we need more research in this area – particularly in relation to causation. However, we can say with some certainty that children who are depressed, left out or disenfranchised – a group that often includes those from deprived social circumstances – are much more likely to buy into the advertising promises that cool stuff will make things better (Opree, Buijzen and Valkenburg 2012). Instead, however, this leads to negativity towards parents and family conflict which in turn actually exacerbates insecurity and low self-esteem – not to mention putting financial pressure on the very families least able to afford it all. It is a vicious circle.

When consumer goods assume too great an importance in the lives of young people this also affects their all-important relationships with their friends, which I discuss in the next section.

BRAND BULLYING

Brands, particularly those associated with fashion and technology, play an important and complex role in the everyday lives of teenagers. As children enter early adolescence they begin to spend less time with their parents and more time with their peers, and with this comes a growing awareness of their own individual identity and how they relate to new social groups. At this age young people have also developed the cognitive capacity to understand the symbolic significance of brands (Chaplin and Roedder 2005), for example, that Gucci represents luxury whilst Primark does not, or that the iPhone 5 has more cachet than the iPhone 4. Given the ubiquity of brand advertising it becomes an almost natural process for teens to incorporate brands and what they represent into their own self-concept and to define themselves in part by the branded clothes they wear and the branded technology they carry around. Psychologists refer to this as 'self-brand connection' (Chaplin and Roedder 2005). Self-brand connections also enable teenagers to signal to others the peer groups they belong to or aspire to belong to, as well as those they wish to dissociate themselves from. As research for the Scottish Parliament found recently, 'Both for boys and girls, having the "right stuff" – in the form of branded goods, with labels and logos clearly displayed – was critically important in terms of self-image and peer group status' (DCSF/DCMS 2009, p.101).

Trainers have come to assume particular symbolic significance, with the choice of brand an important part of teen life. As one 14-year-old explained to an interviewer in a recent study, 'If you got a whole gang of people wearing Lacoste, then you don't wanna rock up wearing Reebok' (Isaksen and Roper 2010, p.142).

One of the reasons wearing the 'right' brand of trainers (in this case Lacoste and definitely not Reebok) or other highly visible personal apparel matters so much is because part of the psychology of contemporary youth appears to involve the feeling of being watched and judged. One teenager was explaining why school uniform can be a great relief to young people because it is not branded, and told the researcher:

> if you're in a place like this with no uniform, like just a t-shirt and a jumper, everyone's always gonna watch what you got on top of your jumper and what you got below…and everyone will always watch. (Isaksen and Roper 2012, p.190)

This living for the gaze of others can create a great deal of pressure, and the term 'style failure' has been used to refer to what happens when a young person does not succeed in having the right brands to fit in (Croghan et al. 2006). Indeed, young people talk of needing brands to bolster their self-esteem and to protect themselves against social exclusion, taunts and teasing (Mayo and Nairn 2009), a feeling that seems to be shared by their parents. In research carried out for the Bailey review (2011) one parent told the interviewers, 'My eldest's school shoes and coat were bought out of us worrying that he may be bullied if it wasn't the right look.'

These comments demonstrate the enormous power wielded by brands. When we stop to think, it is an extraordinary state of affairs when young people (and, indeed, their parents) can feel inadequate without the right products and see their peers as outcasts if they don't have, for example, a tiny crocodile on their shoes. None of this is logical. So why are so many of us victims? Part of it is, of course, the result of massive advertising campaigns that serve to create the impression that ownership of certain brands is quite simply 'normal'. The Apple corporation, for example, spent US$691 million on advertising in 2011 – a sum that it would take the average UK family over 23,000 years to earn (Apple Insider 2010)! What this massive sum buys is ubiquity. We see the Apple brand on our TVs, on our computers, on posters on our streets, in our newspapers, in our magazines, on our buses and trains – everywhere we go. This ubiquity creates what psychologists call 'false consensus' – that is, the mistaken impression that the brand is owned by more people than it actually is (Bennett 1999). Advertising makes us think that everyone has an iPad/iPod/iPhone and that if we don't we are somehow deviant. False consensus about brand ownership causes particular anxiety in young people and manifests itself as a newly identified phenomenon of FOMO (Fear of Missing Out), which now appears in the Urban Dictionary (http://www.urdandictionary.com/define.php?term=Fomo).

For many young people this fear is of more than missing out – it is a very real fear of bullying and the serious psychological consequences that can ensue. A host of studies, examined below, have shown how brands and bullying are intimately entwined and how damaging this can be.

'I've seen kids get bullied because they have a brick for a mobile phone,' was a comment made by a young person in a survey by the Children's Commissioner and the youth group Amplify (Children's Commissioner for England and Amplify 2011) whilst other research has shown that some children refuse to speak to others if they are not wearing an 'acceptable' brand of trainers (Elliot and Leonard 2004). Teachers are noticing this in schools across the country and in a study by the Association of Teachers and Lecturers (ATL) almost half of teachers answered 'yes' to the question, 'Have children or young people who cannot afford fashion items and/or branded goods been excluded, isolated or bullied by their peers?' (ATL 2008). Dr Mary Bousted, General Secretary of the ATL, concluded that, 'It is incredibly sad to hear how many youngsters are bullied or isolated for not having the same clothes or accessories as their classmates…schools and colleges should be places where all children feel equal.'

A study by the National Foundation for Educational Research (NFER) (Benton 2011) highlighted, 'the potential harm done to young people when they experience bullying through "being left out"', which is exactly the sort of bullying that arises from brand victimisation. The report made the damning comment that, 'This type of bullying is more strongly associated with poor emotional well-being than any other type including more explicit forms such as physical or verbal abuse' (p.6).

The Good Childhood Report 2012 by The Children's Society (2012) also surveyed the relationships between peer pressure, bullying and children's well-being, and found that peer pressure and no longer being friends with someone were very closely associated with poor well-being, and that bullying, 'has as much power to explain variations in well-being as all the individual and family characteristics included in the survey combined' (p.33).

This report also found that 39 per cent of children who did not have 'the right kind of clothes to fit in with other people your age', were unhappy with their appearance compared with only 13 per cent of those who did have the 'right' clothes. Moreover, there was a clear link between the number of material items a child had (such as brand name trainers, iPod, etc.) and their satisfaction with their appearance.

It is clear then that brands have the power to drive wedges not only between families but also between friends, and we have seen that 'brand bullying' centres on the victimisation of children who do not have the most heavily advertised clothes and gadgets. Yet this story has another part and that is the role that income inequality plays in the self-brand connections that have become vital social currency for our youth. It is to this that we turn next.

THOSE WHO HAVE LESS WANT MORE

We saw earlier in the chapter that licensed toys cost considerably more than unlicensed toys and, of course, desirable brands also charge a premium. A pair of UGG boots, for example, costs around £100 whereas a remarkably similar pair with no logo bought from Topshop, for example, will only set you back about £10 or £20.

The brands with big margins naturally have a big budget for advertising and we have seen that a big advertising budget buys the belief amongst consumers that a brand is ubiquitous and 'cool'. Ownership of desirable brands thus comes to symbolise – subtly and imperceptibly – not only that you belong to the cool group but also that you have enough money to afford them. Brand symbolism and brand bullying are therefore connected not just with social identity but also with economic identity. We can see this in the following comments made by a girl from an economically disadvantaged home in Sweden. She is talking about a clique at her school that is known – through its affinity to the designer brand Chloe – as 'The Chloe Gang': 'The Chloe Gang likes expensive things…they think they are the best! They say – I'm the best, I'm better than you and I have expensive things… They have real UGGs!' (Nain *et al.* 2011, p.60).

The resentment is palpable and we can see how brand bullying involves not only rivalry between 'in groups' and 'out groups' but also discrimination between rich and poor. Being part of this gang signifies your ability to afford expensive brands and 'real UGGs'. Sweden is one of the most equal countries in the world, with a low gap between the lowest and highest incomes. This begs the question as to what these dynamics are like in the UK where there is a greater gap between rich and poor than at any time since 1854, the year that Charles Dickens wrote *Hard Times* (see Dorling 2011). Almost 30 per cent of children live in impoverished families – that means 3.8 million children (CPAG 2012). What does brand symbolism mean to them?

It is well documented that children from low-income families watch more TV than their affluent counterparts as it is a cheap form of entertainment in comparison with, for example, joining sports or music clubs, which often require expensive transport and equipment (Nairn *et al.* 2007). We have seen above that heavier TV watching is strongly associated with more purchase requests and a greater tendency to hold materialistic values, which in turn is associated with stress in the household. In families where lack of money already contributes to a stressful atmosphere, it is clear that advertising can exacerbate this. We also know that UK teenagers use brands as a kind of shield against the stigma of poverty that exists in unequal societies. A teenager interviewed for the Children's Commissioner's research, when asked why children and young people feel pressure to own certain brands, replied that it is 'because everyone else seems to have them and none of us wants to look poor'. Her friend agreed, 'anything to prove you've got money' (Children's Commissioner for England 2011).

The views of the young people in a completely separate study talking about the Lacoste and Reebok trainers whose voices we heard earlier in the chapter concur, 'Yeah, if you came in plain white trainers you're more likely to get bullied...like they think you're poor' (Isaksen and Roper 2008).

These findings have been echoed across many studies over the past few years, all of which point to the intense pressure on young people from poor backgrounds to fit into the contemporary consumer culture and the pivotal role of brands in this endeavour. Elliot and Leonard, for example, note in their 2004 landmark study of children in a very deprived community in the UK, 'If a child is wearing branded trainers they are seen as popular and able to fit in with their peers. These opinions are so strongly held that the children would prefer to talk to someone wearing branded trainers than unbranded trainers' (Elliot and Leonard 2004, p.347).

Isaksen and Roper (2008), in a study of another deprived group, go further, concluding that:

> an inability to 'keep up' with the latest fashion trends (due to restricted consumption opportunities) may result in a damaged self-concept amongst low-income teenagers, which leads to heightened susceptibility to consumption pressures and hence heightens the negative socio-psychological impacts of living in poverty. (p.1063)

They identify a vicious circle where teenagers' self-esteem is damaged by not being able to afford the cool brands, which in turn makes these brands even more desirable, leading to inevitable financial problems as they are often simply not affordable. Isaksen and Roper go on to argue in a later paper that self-esteem has become 'commodified', that is, something that can be bought and sold with disadvantaged young people desperately trying to 'buy' self-worth by spending money they don't have on heavily advertised brands (Isaksen and Roper 2012). This is corroborated by a 14-year-old in the UNICEF UK study (Nairn *et al.* 2011) who told the researchers that the current youth climate is such in contemporary UK society that, 'You can live in a dustbin but as long as you've got a Blackberry or an iPod, you're accepted.'

This is a damning indictment of our society in which, through the eyes of our children, what we own is more important than social justice. So what can those working with children and young people do to try to counteract some of these effects?

HELPING CHILDREN AND YOUNG PEOPLE NAVIGATE THE COMMERCIAL WORLD

We have seen in this chapter how advertising and branding interacts in subtle and complex ways with a number of facets of children's well-being, but there are things we can do to help children build resilience.

- The first is for adults to get to grips with new advertising techniques, particularly those using new media, so that we can help children navigate them and understand their intentions. The organisation Media Smart (www.mediasmart.org.uk) has prepared a *Digital Media Pack* especially for parents to explain digital advertising techniques and it has also created a version of *The Game of Life*, which allows children to understand how advertising is created. These tools can help open up conversations about consumer pressure and how it affects relationships with family and friends. Getting young people to critically appraise commercial activities is a step towards building up resistance to pressure.

- The Bailey review found that parents felt they could not make their voices heard and lacked the confidence to complain about commercial activities they didn't like. In response the media regulators have created ParentPort (www.parentport.org.uk), which provides a central internet portal explaining where to go to complain about advertising, retailing, video games, films and TV programmes. We can encourage both parents and children to use this when they see something they don't like and to feel emboldened to assert their voices.

- The National Trust has joined together with a number of other organisations around the publication of its *Natural Childhood* report (Moss 2012), which is trying to get children and their parents involved in simple, free-of-charge outdoor activities such as going for a walk, which can create family bonds as well as getting children away from screen-based, commercially sponsored entertainment.

- At a more fundamental level, commercial pressures on young people will be less extreme in a more equal society. Policies such as the Living Wage supported by UNICEF UK are likely to help, as are more radical ideas such as salary capping.

- Above all, we need to engage young people in the debate over the commercialisation of childhood so that they can continue to challenge big business and the effects it has on their well-being.

REFERENCES

Apple Insider (2010) 'Apple's 2010 ad budget increases by $190 million, but still outpaced by new sales growth.' Available at: http://appleinsider.com/articles/10/10/27/apples_2010_ad_budget_increases_by_190_million_but_still_outpaced_by_new_sales_growth, accessed on 4 July 2013.

ATL (Association of Teachers and Lecturers) (2008) 'Children are highly influenced by brands and logos.' London: ATL. Available at www.atl.org.uk/media-office/media-archive/children-influenced-brands-logos-ATL.asp, accessed on 22 October 2012.

Bailey, R. (2011) *Letting Children Be Children. An Independent Review of the Commercialisation and Sexualisation of Children.* London: Department of Education.

Barnes, B. (2012) 'Theme park income spurs profits at Disney.' *The New York Times*, 7 February. Available at http://mediadecoder.blogs.nytimes.com/2012/02/07/theme-park-income-spurs-profits-at-disney, accessed on 3 November 2012.

Bennett, R. (1999) 'Sports sponsorship, spectator recall and false consensus.' *European Journal of Marketing, 33*, 3/4, 291–313.

Benton, T. (2011) *Sticks and Stones May Break My Bones But Being Left on My Own Is Worse: An Analysis of Reported Bullying at School Within NFER Attitude Surveys.* November. Slough: National Foundation for Educational Research. Available at www.nfer.ac.uk/nfer/publications/ASUR01/ASUR01.pdf, accessed on 14 June 2010.

Block, A.B. (2012) 'Robert Iger to Wall Street: Disney bought Lucasfilm for "Star Wars".' *The Hollywood Reporter*, 30 October. Available at www.hollywoodreporter.com/news/robert-iger-wall-street-disney-384543, accessed on 3 November 2012.

Branigan, T. (2012) 'Chinese parents defrauded by "perfect" education.' *The Guardian*, 28 August. Available at www.guardian.co.uk/world/2012/aug/28/parents-china-education-children-course, accessed on 4 November 2010.

Buckingham, D., Willett, R., Bragg, S. and Russell, R. (2010) *External Research on Sexualised Goods Aimed at Children. Report to the Scottish Parliament Equal Opportunities Committee.* Scottish Parliament Paper 374. Edinburgh: Scottish Parliament.

Buijzen, M. and Valkenburg, P. (2003) 'The unintended effects of television advertising: a parent-child survey.' *Communication Research, 30,* 483–503.

Chaplin, L. and Roedder, J.D. (2005) 'The development of self-brand connections in children.' *Journal of Consumer Research, 32,* 1, June, 119–129.

Children's Commissioner for England (2011) *'Trying to Get By': Consulting with Children and Young People on Child Poverty.* London: Office of the Children's Commissioner. Available at www.childrenscommissioner.gov.uk/content/publications/content_480, accessed on 22 October 2012.

Children's Commissioner for England and Amplify (2011) *Children, Young People and the Commercial World. Response to the Bailey Review Call for Evidence.* London: Office of the Children's Commissioner. Available at www.childrenscommissioner.gov.uk/content/publications, accessed on 16 May 2013.

Children's Society, The (2012) *The Good Childhood Report 2012: A Review of Our Children's Well-being.* Leeds: The Children's Society. Available at www.childrenssociety.org.uk/what-we-do/research/well-being/good-childhood-report-2012, accessed on 22 October 2012.

CPAG (Child Poverty Action Group) (2012) 'Child poverty facts and figures.' London: CPAG. Available at www.cpag.org.uk/child-poverty-facts-and-figures, accessed on 4 November 2012.

Croghan, R., Griffin, C., Hunter, J. and Phoenix, A. (2006) 'Style failure: consumption, identity and social exclusion.' *Journal of Youth Studies, 9,* 4, 463–478.

DCSF/DCMS (2009) *The Impact of the Commercial World on Children's Wellbeing: Report of an Independent Assessment.*

Dorling, D. (2011) *Injustice: Why Social Inequality Persists.* Bristol: The Policy Press.

Elliot, R. and Leonard, C. (2004) 'Peer pressure and poverty: Exploring fashion brands and consumption symbolism among children of the "British poor".' *Journal of Consumer Behaviour, 3,* 4, 347–359.

Isaksen, K. (2010) *The Impacts of the Consumer Culture and Prolific Branding on British Adolescents: A Vicious Cycle? A Comparison between High and Low-Income Adolescents.* A thesis submitted to The University of Manchester for the degree of Doctor of Philosophy in the Faculty of Humanities.

Isaksen, K.J. and Roper, S. (2008) 'The impact of branding on low-income adolescents: A vicious cycle?' *Psychology and Marketing, 25,* 11, 1063–1087.

Isaksen, K.J. and Roper, S. (2012) 'The commodification of self-esteem: branding and British teenagers.' *Psychology and Marketing, 29,* 3, 117–135.

Lindstrom, M. and Seybold, P.B. (2003) *Brandchild: Remarkable Insights into the Minds of Today's Global Kids and Their Relationships with Brands*. London: Kogan Page.

Liverpool Victoria Friendly Society (2012) *Cost of a Child. From Cradle to College 2012*. Liverpool: Liverpool Victoria Friendly Society.

Mayo, E. and Nairn, A. (2009) *Consumer Kids: How Big Business is Grooming Our Children for Profit*. London: Constable & Robinson.

Moss, S. (2012) *Natural Childhood*. Swindon: National Trust. Available at www.nationaltrust.org.uk/document-1355766991839, accessed on 4 November 2012.

Nairn, A., Ormrod, J. and Bottomley, P. (2007) *Watching, Wanting and Well-being: Exploring the Links. A Study of 9-13 year olds in England and Wales*. London: National Consumer Council.

Nairn, A., Duffy, B., Sweet, O., Swiecicka, J. and Pope, S. (2011) *Children's Wellbeing in the UK, Sweden and Spain: The Role of Inequality and Materialism*. London: UNICEF UK/Ipsos MORI Social Research Unit.

NPD Group (2012) 'Licensed toy sales in the United States experienced growth in first quarter of 2012.' Available at https://www.npd.com/wps/portal/npd/us/news/press-releases/pr_120509.

Opree, S., Buijzen, M. and Valkenburg, P. (2012) 'Low life satisfaction increases materialism in children who are frequently exposed to advertising.' *Paediatrics, 130*, 3, 486–491.

Play England (2008) *Survey by Play England*. London: Playday. Available at www.playengland.org.uk, accessed on 4 November 2012.

Schor, J.B. (2004) *Born to Buy: The Commericalized Child and the New Consumer Culture*. New York: Scribner.

Smithers, R. (2012) 'Cost of raising a child rises to £218,000.' *The Guardian*, 26 January. Available at www.guardian.co.uk/money/2012/jan/26/cost-raising-child-rises-218000, accessed on 3 November 2012.

CHAPTER 3

CHILD OBESITY AND THE JUNK FOOD MARKETEERS

TIM LOBSTEIN

This chapter describes how the food industry encourages over-consumption of junk food, with children as its primary target. It looks at the four areas of product marketing (price, product place and promotion) and discusses what might be done to protect children.

Before getting too deeply into this topic I would like to offer some context.

First, junk food promotion is not the only cause of the substantial rise in the numbers of overweight children in the last three decades. Children were exposed to some forms of junk food promotion before this period but did not consume the high levels of soft drinks, confectionery, snacks and sugary cereals that are eaten by children now, possibly because the prices of those foods were relatively high, compared with income levels and compared with the price of alternative, healthier foods. Equally, some children nowadays are overweight without being exposed to junk food advertising: children under two years old will have had little exposure to advertising, but this age group has followed the national trend for rising obesity levels. For such young children other factors are playing a part: for example, what the parents are eating, how this might affect the growth of the foetus, the use of formula milks instead of breastfeeding, the use of commercial weaning foods and other factors that affect the growth and health of infants.

There are also non-commercial influences on the dietary patterns of children, amongst which school meals and school food environments rightly play a significant part. After the UK school meals standards were abandoned in the early 1980s the quality of meals began to decline, and only in the early 2000s has the quality started to improve again – thanks to years of dedicated action by parents and health campaigners, and a champion in the form of celebrity chef Jamie Oliver. Additionally, overweight is not simply a result of dietary intake but is also promoted by physical inactivity, which in turn is a response to changing entertainment patterns, increased use of cars and other social trends that reduce the need for physical exertion and encourage sitting for prolonged periods.

MARKETING JUNK FOOD

However, among the many influences in a child's environment that encourage overweight, perhaps the one that embeds the best-planned and best-funded assault on children's health, undertaken entirely for private gain and subject to poor regulation and oversight, is the commercial promotion of junk food.

By 'commercial promotion' we mean the four 'Ps' of commercial marketing: Price, Product, Place and Promotion. In all four cases there have been significant developments in the last few decades in the targeting of children with the least nutritious, most disease-promoting products. We shall have a brief look at the first three and then a longer look at the fourth, the deliberate promotional marketing of junk food products towards children.

PRICE

While confectionery companies have for many years exploited the 'pocket money' market by providing 'penny sweets' in small packets or sold loose, in lurid colours and startling flavours, the last two decades have seen this approach extended to savoury snacks in small portions, and to low-cost soft drinks, also sold in smaller, ready-to-consume packs. Corner newsagents put these 'treats' at children's eye levels and hand-grabbing levels. Sadly, the low price is matched by the low nutritional quality in virtually every case.

Caterers have also seen the potential to sell cheaper products expressly designed to appeal to children's love of fats and sugar.

All too frequently, service stations, steakhouse chains and pubs offer 'children's menus' that feature the lowest common denominators: chicken nuggets, fish fingers, chips, chips, chips. Again, low price and low nutritional quality, aimed at children.

The reason why low nutritional quality and low price seem to go together is not immediately obvious, as low prices for a carrot, an apple or a banana would surely argue for a better range of pocket money treats and children's menu items. The trouble is that fresh foods tend to be perishable, and perishable means that they go off before they have been sold and the profit vanishes. What a grocer or caterer wants are products with long shelf lives, which are not damaged in transport, do not fade or dry out and can be prepared for service without any skill. Mass-produced foods are the thing, and they have come to dominate the food supply. As sales rise, the unit price gets cheaper, and sales rise still further. Figure 4.1 below shows how prices for healthier foods have shot ahead of the overall price paid for food eaten at home, while prices for less healthy foods have become relatively cheaper over the last two decades, 1992–2010.

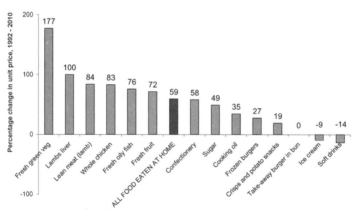

Figure 4.1 UK price changes in foods, 1992–2010
Source: UK Government family food statistics 2012 and previous years

PRODUCT

As the previous section indicated, the nutritional quality of foods targeting children at the very cheapest end of the range is poor, to the point of encouraging dental disease, liver disease, heart disease, diabetes and obesity.

Similar comments can be made about other products – not necessarily the cheapest – that are designed specifically for children, both in the retail and the catering sectors. Fast food restaurants have promoted children's foods for many years, often using free toys along with cartoon characters and packaging that is attractive to children. This isn't the place to discuss the quality of fast food meals, although it is interesting to note that, when the health authorities in the city of San Francisco banned fast food stores from giving free toys with meals unless the meals exceeded a stated minimum level of good nutritional quality, McDonald's started charging one cent for a toy with a meal, rather than meet the nutritional quality required (*Huffington Post* 2011).

However, most children eat food at home, and most of that food is bought from shops and supermarkets. A survey of UK food products sold in supermarkets and packaged with labels that were especially attractive to children or indicated that the food was intended for children found that the majority were of poor nutritional quality (Branca, Nikogosian and Lobstein 2007). The survey used the UK Government's criteria for 'red' traffic light labelling, and found that, of 368 children's food products (excluding soft drinks, snacks and products for special occasions):

- sixteen per cent were high in fat

- thirty per cent were high in saturated fat

- forty-six per cent were high in salt

- fifty-seven per cent were high in sugar

- seventy-seven per cent were high in at least one of the above.

PLACE

Over more than 20 years of campaigning by parent groups, consumer groups and health organisations to ban the promotion of sweets and snacks at shop tills and checkouts, the big supermarket chains have made and broken a series of promises. 'Chuck Sweets Off the Check-Out' in the 1980s achieved a number of promises from the big retailers to introduce a minimum number of sweet-free checkouts in every store. By the end of the 1990s the number of families using supermarkets for their daily shopping had increased, but the sweet-free checkouts had largely disappeared and, worse, a range of fatty and salty snacks had joined the sweets at the checkout. New campaigns have led to some improvements, with some supermarkets offering some checkouts free of sweets and snacks, but at the same time soft drinks have joined the junk foods at the till.

The theory behind the sale of such foods at the till is that consumers can be suckers for impulse purchasing – the almost unconscious reaction to pick up something attractive while your thoughts are focused on checking your shopping list or finding your purse. The companies know that items should be small, attractive, familiar and tasty or else the impulse may not work. To get children involved, the impulse products need to be a lower height – preferably within the arm's reach of a buggy-pushed child, whose firm grasp of a product leads to a predictable struggle, just as the parent reaches the till. A fight between public health campaigners and supermarkets has been converted into a fight between a parent and their child, but the winner is the supermarket all the same.

PROMOTION

While TV advertising to children is tolerated in most countries (notable exceptions are Sweden and the Canadian province of Québec), the media channels and promotional settings available to food marketeers have expanded dramatically in the last two decades. The following lists show just some of the opportunities for promoting junk food to children.

PLACEMENT OF ONLINE ADVERTISING

• On search engines.

• On social networking sites.

• On news sites, music sites and blogs.

• Around or on TV-on-demand.

• Around or in films and media clips viewed online.

- Around or in online and downloadable games, music and other media.
- On company websites or company-owned dedicated children's sites.

PRODUCT PLACEMENT AND BRANDING

- Product placement in TV scheduled programmes, radio programmes, films, computer games, downloadable apps.
- Branded books, for example, counting books for pre-schoolers.
- Branded toys, for example, fast food store as a playhouse.

BRANDED COMPUTER GAMES

- Interactive company-owned websites, for example, with puzzles and games including branded objects.
- Branding on sports teams and advertising at sports and cultural events.
- Branding on school equipment and sports kits.

VIRAL MARKETING

- Word-of-mouth and personal recommendation by consumers, sometimes in return for payment or reward, and increasingly encouraged in social networking sites (Tripodi 2012).

SPONSORSHIP

- Sponsorship of TV and radio programmes, music videos.
- Celebrity product endorsement.
- Sponsorship of community and school events and contests.
- Corporate gifts of educational materials and equipment.
- Corporate support of 'health' campaigns, sports clubs, school meals.

DIRECT MARKETING

- Promotional emails.

- Promotional sales by telephone, text messaging to mobile phones.

- Promotion and sampling schemes in schools.

ADVERGAMING

- Branding and advertising embedded in video games and interactive fantasy worlds, available online or for downloading. The users may provide their contact details to marketers in return for multiplayer interactive gaming and opportunities for rewards.

POINT OF SALE AND PRODUCT PROMOTION

- Packaging vouchers linked to discounts on videos, films, music.

- Packaging codes link to online games, social networking sites or downloadable apps.

- Vending machine codes link to online immediate discounts.

INTEGRATED MARKETING

- This includes linking film, toy and food products, and now also including new media, for example, a breakfast cereal that has on-pack promotion of a brand-promoting game, which is played on a website, with matching Facebook page and Twitter messaging. The game can be played interactively with other people worldwide, and is downloadable as an app to play on a smartphone.

INTERACTIVE AND USER-GENERATED MARKETING

- This includes two-way marketing and market-shaping activities, for example, TV adverts invite viewers to vote for different flavours of a brand, which then gets produced and marketed. In another example, the company launches a competition to create a video commercial, which individuals then put on YouTube for viral distribution.

In each case these are conscious decisions by food company researchers, designers and psychologists, using taste trials, eye-tracking, focus groups and consumer taste-test panels. Growing sections of the advertising industry are devoted to the development of material and techniques for capturing and exploiting children's natural curiosity and interest in eating. An estimate of the commercial activities of the world's food industries in 2001 found that their advertising budget was some US$40 billion (Lang and Millstone 2002). To put this figure in context, it is greater than the entire economy (Gross Domestic Product) of Romania or Bangladesh or any one of 145 other national economies, that same year.

Advertising on internet sites has rapidly increased in the last decade. In the UK the budget for internet advertising of all products exceeded that for TV advertising in 2009, having risen from under £200 million in 2002 to nearly £5 billion in 2010 (Phillipson 2009).

Data on children's access to the internet are available for some countries: figures from the UK in 2011 show that 65 per cent of children aged 5–7 were accessing the internet through home computers, rising to 85 per cent of UK children aged 8–11 (Ofcom 2011). These figures indicate that UK children's access to and use of the internet has risen some 30 per cent during a four-year period 2007–11.

Some food company websites offer fantasy games and cartoons targeting children, and even show videos of adverts that would likely break the law if they were to be shown during children's TV in countries such as the UK and Sweden.

PROMOTING BRAND LOYALTY

Companies also develop their own websites to increase brand awareness and consumer loyalty, but these activities are not usually defined as advertising and may not be included in estimates of advertising expenditure. Food companies' homepages give children an opportunity to engage with the brand (for example, become a 'fan'). Further involvement comes when the companies' websites provide social contexts that display the names of a user's friends who are already 'fans' of the brand (Nielsen and Facebook 2010).

With 56,000 new fans joining it daily, Coca-Cola's fan page was rated as number 11 in the world in mid-2011, with a total of nearly 32 million fans (Sekander 2011). It was the only food brand with such a high ranking – the next-placed food-related brand being Starbucks, which attracted 23 million fans, having gained 13 million in a year (Walsh 2010).

A recent development for food companies is to promote their brand using advergames (digital games or fantasy worlds with in-built advertising or branding). Most major food companies have developed game-playing and fantasy video sites for young children.[1] In the USA McDonald's advergames attracted over 4 million unique child visitors and a further 3.5 million unique teenage visitors in 2009 (Harris, Schwartz and Brownell 2010). Games include prompts for users to order home-delivery food while playing the game.

Sites that offer social gaming (multi-player online games) are expected to grow rapidly; although the games may or may not have embedded advertising, the sites can include banner advertising and other marketing messages showing the brand. Figures from the USA indicate that advertisers spent an estimated US$192 million advertising on social game sites in 2011, a 60 per cent increase over 2010 and predicted to rise a further 40 per cent in 2012 (eMarketer Digital Intelligence 2011a).

INTERACTING WITH EACH CHILD

Besides passive advertising, food companies have become 'part of the conversation' using digital marketing to create, test and adjust their marketing messages in real time, with young people learning about new products, evaluating them and providing feedback to the companies (Montgomery et al. 2011). A further valuable and low cost marketing method is to encourage young people to download or record a commercial and then distribute it to their friends or place it on a social media site for free access. This is termed 'user-generated' marketing, and its distribution is termed

---

1   Examples at the time of writing this report include (all accessed 24 June 2012):
   • www.nestlecrunch.com/playground.aspx
   • http://city.haribo.com
   • www.nesquik.com/kids/games/index.aspx
   • www.ricekrispies.com/en_us/pick-a-card.html.

'viral' as it relies on users to spread the messages informally. In so far as a company has no involvement in the spread of the commercial message, the company can deny responsibility over who is exposed and what effect it has.

Companies increasingly design their marketing campaigns to involve a variety of media and devices. Interactive media allow companies to gather information and refine their marketing approach to target the profile of their material to suit the individual viewer. Social networking sites such as Facebook and messaging services such as Twitter are popular with children and young people and therefore with advertisers. Social media marketing can increase advertisement recall, awareness of the product or brand and purchase intent (Nielsen and Facebook 2010). Global expenditure on advertising on social networking sites reached an estimated US$5.5 billion in 2011 and is predicted to reach US$10 billion annually by 2013 (eMarketer Digital Intelligence 2011b). Estimates from France and Spain indicate that online advertising now accounts for some 13–15 per cent of all media advertising, and is due to rise to 20 per cent by 2014 (von Abrams 2010). Combined exposure to TV and internet social networking is also increasing: over 50 per cent of *X Factor* viewers in the UK reportedly used the Facebook site at the same time as they were watching the TV show (Calladine 2011).

An additional tool for marketeers is online behavioural tracking, in which the company monitors individuals' personal interests and then advertises selected products that might interest them. By analysing children's social network and social groups, the companies can directly select messages to individual children and to linked groups of children and their social community (Montgomery *et al.* 2011). The average UK teenager has over 450 Facebook 'friends' and the average UK young adult has over 1000 'friends' (Intersperience 2011).

While in theory Facebook is used only by children over the age of 13, in reality, evidence from the UK (Ofcom 2011) indicates that among eight-year-olds, one child in 12 has a social media page (most often on Facebook). Among children aged nine, this rises to one child in every seven. The effect is that children this young are exposed to marketing methods and messages designed for older children (and within five years or so, designed specifically for adults).

MARKETING ON THE MOVE

The use of mobile phones has become widespread among teenage children. Data from the UK show that use of a smartphone (mobile phone with internet access) is common among relatively young age groups: among children aged 8–11, one in eight owns a smartphone, and among children aged 5–7, a remarkable one in 50 owns a smartphone (Ofcom 2011).

As with email marketing, messages can be customised to known users' interests and the responses tracked. As reported by comScore in September 2010, almost half of European mobile users received advertising via text messages (comScore 2010). This communication can be interactive, as customers can communicate with food companies: for example, Coca-Cola's new 'cashless' vending machines encourage mobile phone payment, and when the customer sends a message to the company that includes a vending machine code, the customer receives a discount that comes directly to the vending machine as they make the purchase (Coca-Cola 2011). Simultaneously, the company gains a phone number belonging to a person known to be a purchaser of the product.

Smartphones have also created a new opportunity for marketing through 'apps' (downloadable software applications). Mobile apps allow food companies to communicate information about products and help consumers to find a company's products in stores (for example, Kraft's iFood Assistant app), order their products for home delivery (for example, Pizza Hut app), or send discounts and coupons (for example, Grocery IQ iPhone app) (Pitt *et al.* 2011).

PARENTS NOT IN THE EQUATION?

Whatever the rhetoric of the food companies and politicians who urge parents to be more responsible about the food children eat, and the TV they watch, the reality is that children are directly targeted by advertisers with little or no opportunity for parents to intervene. That parents should be held responsible for their children's health is not a discussion for this chapter, but that parent's assumed responsibility is being undermined by direct contact between the junk food advertisers and the child is a matter of considerable concern.

The issue has been recognised for many years. In 1874, the English Parliament passed the Infants' Relief Act to protect children under the age of 21, 'from their own lack of experience and from the wiles of pushing tradesmen and moneylenders' (James 1965). The Act, which absolved parents from their children's debts, is one of the earliest governmental policies to address children's unique vulnerability to commercial exploitation.

Despite the increasing evidence demonstrating the links between children's exposure to food marketing messages and consequential changes in dietary behaviour, the protection of children has become weaker as new and rapidly expanding forms of media become available to larger numbers of children, and companies take advantage of these low-cost, effective means of reaching children directly.

TIME FOR STRONGER RULES

The advertisers are aware that they are coming in for criticism and have come up with a number of voluntary 'self-regulation' proposals to avoid the imposition of statutory regulation. These differ in different countries, and in some cases the voluntary industry measures supplement local, stronger regulation, and in other cases they are the only protection for children being offered.

Such voluntary, self-regulation, however, is easily reversed when the pressure is off, and even at its best suffers from distinct drawbacks (see below).

WHY THE FOOD INDUSTRY'S SELF-REGULATORY CODES ARE NOT GOOD ENOUGH

Campaigning organisations and parents' groups have been critical of the voluntary measures being offered by the food industry. In particular they state that:

1. The codes themselves are seriously flawed, in that they:
   - are complex and difficult to understand and to monitor
   - differ from country to country and region to region
   - do not apply to all food advertisers, only those that say they will abide by the codes

- only cover advertising content that is 'directed primarily to children' rather than all the advertising seen by children
- do not prevent unhealthy food advertising during TV programmes watched by the greatest number of children
- do not cover all the forms of media that children use
- do not cover all age groups of children
- consider one advertisement at a time, and not the cumulative or compound effects of similar types of advertisements
- use criteria for deciding what is healthy/unhealthy that suit the companies, allowing many unhealthy foods to be advertised.

2. The administration and enforcement of the codes are grossly inadequate because:

- the schemes rely on complaints from the public
- the decisions often give the benefit of doubt to the companies
- the decisions are usually made long after the advertising campaign has finished
- the penalties are small and easily afforded by a food advertiser
- there is no independent monitoring to show that self-regulation has reduced children's exposure to unhealthy food advertising
- there are no controls over advertising entering a country from outside the jurisdiction, for example, via satellite channels or via off-shore internet sites.

The UK is one of the few countries to have introduced legally enforceable controls on advertising of junk food to children, but these controls have weaknesses and gaps. The controls for TV only apply to children's dedicated channels and to programmes with at least 20 per cent of the audience aged under 16, so programmes watched by large numbers of children and also very large numbers of adults (such as soaps and sports) are not included in the controls. Second, the controls for internet have been introduced recently, but do not apply to websites based outside the UK or to brand messages that do not actually say the product should be purchased – such brand messaging is not deemed to be 'advertising' in a strict sense. Mobile phones, smart apps and social media sites are not covered at all – and that is just where the advertisers are focusing their new campaigns.

From the industry's view, the fatter we all are the better. Fatter people eat more, and eating more is good for the food business. The earlier we get fat the longer we will be eating excess food. But the politicians and advertisers who defend the free market economy are sacrificing our children's health. They know what they are doing, whatever they might say, and so we have to make it clear that we are holding them accountable.

We know what they are doing. And although it is a struggle to organise against the food companies' worst behaviour, we owe it to our children to do whatever we can.

TAKING ACTION

There is no point reading this chapter and getting anxious. Nor is it enough to convert your anxiety into anger. What is needed is to harness the anger and get active. There are loads of campaigns, parents' organisations, school groups, trade unions and professional associations that want to protect children from the marketing tricks of the food and soft drink industries. Here are a couple of places to start:

- In the UK: www.sustainweb.org/childrensfoodcampaign.

- In the USA: www.cspinet.org/about/index.html (and their site www.foodmarketing.org).

- In Australia: www.parentsjury.org.au and www.opc.org.au.

REFERENCES

Branca, F., Nikogosian, H. and Lobstein, T. (2007) *The Challenge of Obesity in the WHO European Region and the Strategies for Response.* Copenhagen: World Health Organization. Available at www.euro.who.int/__data/assets/pdf_file/0010/74746/E90711.pdf, accessed on 22 April 2013.

Calladine, D. (2011) '12 trends for 2012.' *Aegis Media.* Available at www.slideshare.net/NextGenerationMedia/12-trends-for-2012, accessed on 22 April 2013.

Coca-Cola (2011) *Google Showcase Cashless Vending with Bi-Coastal Event.* Atlanta, GA: The Coca-Cola Company. Available at www.coca-colacompany. com/press-center/company-articles/coca-cola-google-showcase-cashless-vending-with-bi-coastal-event, accessed on 22 April 2013.

comScore (2010) 'More than 100 million mobile consumers in EU5 received SMS advertising.' Press release. Available at www.comscore.com/layout/ set/popup/layout/set/popup/Press_Events/Press_Releases/2010/11/ More_Than_100_Million_Mobile_Consumers_in_EU5_Received_SMS_ Advertising, accessed on 22 April 2013.

eMarketer Digital Intelligence (2011a) 'Social gaming market to surpass $1 billion.' *eMarketer,* 12 January. Available at www.emarketer.com/Article. aspx?R=1008166, accessed on 22 April 2013.

eMarketer Digital Intelligence (2011b) 'Social network ad revenues to reach $10 billion worldwide in 2013.' *eMarketer,* 5 October. Available at www. emarketer.com/Article/Social-Network-Ad-Revenues-Reach-10-Billion-Worldwide-2013/1008625, accessed on 22 April 2013.

Harris, J., Schwartz, M. and Brownell, K. (2010) *Evaluating Fast Food Nutrition and Marketing to Youth.* Newhaven, CT: Yale Rudd Center for Food Policy and Obesity. Available at http://fastfoodmarketing.org/media/FastFoodFACTS_ Report.pdf, accessed on 22 April 2013.

Huffington Post (2011) 'San Francisco Happy Meal toy ban takes effect, sidestepped by McDonald's.' 1 December. Available at www.huffingtonpost. com/2011/11/30/san-francisco-happy-meal-ban_n_1121186.html, accessed on 22 April 2013.

Intersperience (2011) 'Twenty-somethings top online friends' league table.' Press release, 23 May. Available at www.intersperience.com/news_more.asp?news_ id=34, accessed on 22 April 2013.

James, T.E. (1965) *Children and the Law.* Oxford: Pergamon Press.

Lang, T. and Millstone, E. (eds) (2002) *The Atlas of Food.* London: Earthscan Books.

Montgomery, K., Grier, S., Chester, J. and Dorfman L. (2011) *Food Marketing in the Digital Age: A Conceptual Framework and Agenda for Research.* Washington DC: American University. Available at http://bmsg.org/sites/default/ files/bmsg_report_food_marketing_in_the_digital_age_a_conceptual_ framework_0.pdf, accessed on 22 April 2013.

Nielsen and Facebook (2010) *Advertising Effectiveness: Understanding the Value of a Social Media Impression.* Available at www.iab.net/media/file/ NielsenFacebookValueofSocialMediaImpressions.pdf, accessed on 22 April 2013.

Ofcom (2011) *Children and Parents: Media Use and Attitudes.* London: Ofcom. Available at http://stakeholders.ofcom.org.uk/binaries/research/media-literacy/oct2011/Children_and_parents.pdf, accessed on 22 April 2013.

Phillipson, G. (2009) *UK Online Advertising – The Success Story.* Internet Advertising Bureau. Available at www.slideshare.net/vittorio.pasteris/ uk-online-advertising-the-success-story-by-guy-phillipson, accessed on 7 May 2013.

Pitt, L.F., Parent, M., Junglas, I., Chan, A. and Spyropoulou, S. (2011) 'Integrating the smartphone into a sound environmental information systems strategy: principles, practices and a research agenda.' *The Journal of Strategic Information Systems, 20*, 1, 27–37.

Sekander, Y. (2011) 'World's top 100 most popular facebook fan pages.' Available at www.elevatelocal.co.uk/blog/worlds-top-100-most-popular-facebook-fan-pages-08073648, accessed on 22 April 2013.

Tripodi, J.V. (2012) 'The journey to shared value.' Cannes, Coca-Cola press presentation. Available at http://www.coca-colacompany.com/our-company/the-journey-to-shared-value, accessed on 24 June 2012.

von Abrams, K. (2010) 'Online ad spending buoyant in France and Spain.' Available at www.emarketer.com, accessed on 22 July 2013.

Walsh, M. (2010) 'Starbucks tops 10 million Facebook fans.' *Marketing Daily*, 15 July. Available at www.mediapost.com/publications/article/132008/, accessed on 22 April 2013.

CHAPTER 4

THE SCIENCE OF VIOLENT ENTERTAINMENT

DR WAYNE WARBURTON

There is a long history, across cultures, of boys playing with violence-themed toys such as spears, swords and bows and arrows. To give just one example, historian G.R. Owst (1961) talks about boys in Anglo-Saxon times being recorded as using, 'a burly spear from a ragwort stalk, and of a sedge a sword of war'. However, the effects of such toys are still hotly debated today. On one side is the 'boys will be boys' argument, which suggests that boys playing with violence-themed toys is simply a natural part of growing up. Hence the often stated, 'Look at me – I played with toy guns when I was a kid and it didn't do me any harm.' Some with this view take the argument even further, by suggesting that playing with such toys may help children 'blow off steam' and harmlessly vent aggressive impulses. On the other side are arguments that recognise the role of weapons play in setting gender stereotypes, in normalising aggressive behaviour and in desensitising boys to violence. According to this view, playing with such toys sets up patterns of behaviour that may be unhelpful, and that increase rather than reduce the likelihood of aggressive behaviour.

In this chapter I do not want to enter into the debate about whether or not boys should be playing with violence-themed toys or games. I will not prescribe to parents what is right or wrong for their children – that is a decision for parents to make themselves. Rather, to assist readers in making their own informed decisions, I present the scientific findings about boys and violence-themed entertainments and suggest a possible 'moderate' path that takes into account the known findings.

To this end, we first examine whether boys prefer violence-based toys such as guns and spears, the effects of violent toy play on behaviour, and the impact of playing with violent virtual weapons in video games. We also examine the effect of having a weapons-based controller such as a replica gun in such games. Then we examine the reasons why these effects may occur in terms of human psychology. The chapter concludes with some practical notes for parents and professionals who work with boys. Along the way we also examine boys' development at various ages. Before we begin, however, I would like to start by stressing the positive impacts of play and games, and outlining my overall approach to violence-themed entertainments.

POSITIVE IMPACTS OF PLAY AND GAMES

Play is crucial to children's development (Gonzales-Mena 2008), and rough and tumble play is particularly important for boys (Fletcher, St George and Freeman 2012). Children love to engage with new media and techno toys, and these can have many benefits for children, even quite young children (Warburton and Highfield 2012). It is important to remember the many positive impacts that playing games, playing video games and interacting with media can have for children. These include benefits to cognitive development, language acquisition and socialisation for young children and to peer relationships and identity formation for older children. Toys and video games can teach key skills, can help children manage pain, can be used for exercise and can facilitate helping behaviours (see Warburton and Braunstein 2012 for more details). For this reason, the many benefits of play and games should not be forgotten as we explore their possible negative impacts.

A 'RISK FACTOR' APPROACH

In the debate on the impact of violent video games, an argument I often hear is that people play more of such games now, but there is less violent crime, so violent video games cannot be linked with violent behaviour. This argument assumes, wrongly, that playing such games must be the only factor involved in violent behaviour. No credible researcher in this area would ever make such a claim. In my experience, acts of violence (defined as behaviours that have the aim of causing extreme harm to another) never have a single cause. Rather, they are usually the culmination of a whole range of factors that can put a person at greater risk of violence – aggressive personality, attitudes approving violence, harsh early parenting, trauma, violent peer group norms, poverty, gang membership, being male, low IQ, violent media exposure and type of neighbourhood, just to name a few (see Anderson and Warburton 2012). Each of these is a 'risk factor' for violence, but none is sufficient alone to cause a person to be violent. Instead, the risk of violence increases as the number of risk factors increase. If a person has enough risk factors, these may be sufficient to impel that person to violence in situations that have the right triggers, such as being insulted by another person.

It is also important to separate violence from aggression. Violence is at the extreme end of the aggression spectrum. However, aggressive behaviour can include any manner of hurting another person, including teasing, hitting, smashing their things, spreading rumours, bullying online or in person, saying hurtful things or injuring the person in some other way.

When it comes to boys and violence-themed entertainments, it is important to understand that the research refers to aggressive rather than violent behaviour, and that the risk factor approach applies. Playing with violence-themed toys or games is one factor that can influence child behaviour, but it is one of many influences on a child's life, some of which may put the child at greater risk of aggressive behaviour and some of which may reduce it. Thus, the scientific findings need to be put into context. They should not be over-interpreted as suggesting that playing with violent toys will turn a child into an aggressive monster, but neither should they be under-interpreted. Violent entertainments have a clear impact on boys, and this can be a significant one.

THE IMPACT OF VIOLENCE-THEMED ENTERTAINMENTS ON BOYS

BOYS AND TOYS

Perhaps the first issue we should look at is whether boys do tend to prefer toys and games with violent themes. The research suggests they do. A study of girls' and boys' toys by Blakemore and Centers (2005) found that whereas girls' toys tended to emphasise attractiveness and domesticity, boys' toys were frequently rated as violent, exciting and a little dangerous. This preference for violence-themed toys seems to become pronounced by the age of 4–5 (Hellendoorn and Harinck 1997; Liss 1981), and a clear preference for aggressive play over non-aggressive play appears to begin around the same age, continuing through middle childhood (Benenson, Carder and Geib-Cole 2008).

Boys' preferences have been exploited, and to some extent created, by advertising. One study that has demonstrated this is by Lori Klinger and her colleagues (2001). Children aged 9–11 were asked to rate how aggressive children's advertisements were. Advertisements for boys' toys were consistently rated as having more aggressive content than other advertisements. Interestingly, boy participants rated content as less aggressive than girls. Klinger concluded that boys are specifically targeted with aggressive content in advertising, and that boys may become desensitised to aggressive media content as a result.

One particular type of toy that is heavily marketed to boys is the toy gun. Many boys seem to be fascinated by weapons, and especially by firearms. This is borne out by a 2001 study from Geoffrey Jackman and his colleagues (2001), who allowed 29 groups of 8–12-year-old boys to find a real (unloaded) gun to see what they would do. Although boys from most groups found the gun within 15 minutes, only one boy tried to then inform an adult, and he was mocked by the other two members of his group. Most boys were curious, with boys from 16 of the 21 groups that found the gun handling it, and boys from 10 of these groups actually pulling the trigger, even some who realised the gun was genuine. This study amply demonstrates that many boys are drawn to guns, have trouble distinguishing real from replica weapons and have a tendency to handle guns irresponsibly. This may explain in part the large number of injuries sustained each year by boys playing with replica guns (in one US study, there were 818 reports of toy gun injuries in 1980–81 alone; see Tanz, Christoffel and Sagerman 1985).

Studies that assess the psychological impact of playing with toy guns generally take two forms. Some are experiments that let children play with toy guns or non-violent toys, and then assess their behaviour afterward. Such studies are removed from 'real world' situations, but can remove the possibility of other factors causing the changes in behaviour that are measured. Experiments are therefore used to work out if one thing really causes another. Other studies look at how much children play with toy guns in the real world, and whether there is a correlation with how aggressive or anti-social that child typically is. In this type of study a wide range of 'real world' behaviours can be examined at one time, but the issue of what causes what cannot be determined.

Two studies by Turner and Goldsmith in 1976 are of the first type. They looked at the behaviour of four- and five-year-old children playing with either toy guns, airplanes or their usual toys. In each block of time that toy guns were used, there was a substantial increase in anti-social behaviour (hurting someone, smashing something, breaking a rule, swearing and being nasty, bossy or threatening). In subsequent blocks of play with either airplanes or the child's usual toys, anti-social behaviour reduced, only to spike upwards again when toy gun play was re-introduced.

Another important experiment involved 30 young men (aged 18–22) who either played the game 'Mousetrap' or with a pellet gun for 30 minutes (Klinesmith, Kasser and McAndrew 2006). Those who played with the gun had increased testosterone levels compared with the 'Mousetrap' playing group, and were also significantly more aggressive afterwards. Data analysis suggested that playing with the pellet gun increased testosterone levels, and that this in turn had the effect of increasing aggression.

Watson and Peng (1992) had similar findings, but used the second method. They found that frequent toy gun play at home was linked with a greater preference for violence-themed toys, greater dislike for non-aggressive play and real aggressive behaviour (as opposed to aggressive play). In this study there was a stark difference between boys and girls, with boys being far more aggressive. When the researchers looked at those factors that predicted real aggressive behaviour for the whole group (boys and girls), toy gun play at home, having punishing parents and violent television exposure, were all important. However, when boys were separated from girls, there was only one factor that strongly predicted boys' aggression – toy gun play at home.

Of course, guns are not the only violence-themed toys that boys play with. Swords, bows and arrows, clubs, spears and many other weapon-based toys are common. Research using similar methods has also examined the impact of violence-themed toys generally, and the findings are similar to those for toy guns. Experimental studies have tended to look at pre-school boys and boys aged 5–8. They typically find that after playing with violence-themed toys (compared with toys with helping or neutral themes), boys are rated as being more aggressive (Mendoza 1972; Potts *et al.* 1986), even boys rated as being normally non-aggressive (Feshbach 1956).

An important aspect of violence-themed toys is that they are often the result of merchandising off-shoots to successful television series, movies and video games. They might be laser guns used by space rangers, light sabres and pirate swords used in popular movies, armour worn by action heroes or accessories worn by comic book characters. As such, they are not simply replica weapons, but objects with a history that the child knows well (indeed, knowing about the toy is part of what makes it so desirable in the first place). In addition, the scripts about how to behave with the toy weapons from the relevant cartoons, movies and television series are well known to the boys who watch them. For this reason, one will often see boys use such toys in ways that imitate the original users – the pirates, space rangers, super heroes and villains – even when the characters who model the weapons are violent on-screen.

This is a well-researched phenomenon. Early studies show clearly that children who see a film of a model doing something aggressive with a toy, something the children have never seen before, will imitate that behaviour afterwards (Bandura 1973; Bandura, Ross and Ross 1961, 1963). This is a principle known as 'social learning', and has been demonstrated comprehensively for a large range of social behaviours, not just aggression. Further research has revealed that children are more likely to imitate 'models' who they identify with, who are admired or liked, or who are seen to be rewarded for that particular behaviour (see Bandura 1973). One interesting study also showed that children of 6–7 years are more likely to imitate aggressive behaviours involving toys and actions they have an existing liking for (Slife and Rychlak 1982). Together this research suggests that when toys are linked with on-screen heroes or admired characters who use them for an aggressive purpose, children will imitate that behaviour in their play with that toy, and often act out the 'scripts' that they have learned from the television show or movie (see Huesmann and Kirwil 2007).

The type of play that involves the most identification with screen characters is playing video games. Here, there is a considerable wealth of research for parents and others to draw from.

BOYS AND VIDEO GAMES

Children typically start playing video games just before the age of four (Rideout 2011), and use then accelerates, peaking in hours per week at around the ages of 11–14 (Anderson and Warburton 2012; Rideout, Foehr and Roberts 2010; Warburton and Highfield 2012). Over 90 per cent of boys and girls over eight years play video games (for example, Lenhart *et al.* 2008), but boys play for more hours, outplaying girls about 2.5 hours to one (Rideout *et al.* 2010). Relevant to this chapter, research suggests that the more hours children play video games, the more likely it is that the games will have violent content (Krahé and Möller 2004).

Although many parents are aware that their children are playing video games with violent content, in my experience most are unaware of the degree of violence within the games. To give one example, the game *Grand Theft Auto* is rated M17+ in the US, but was played by 56 per cent of US children aged 8–18 in the last big survey (Rideout *et al.* 2010). Apart from the obvious implications regarding the ineffectiveness of the classification system, there are clear developmental implications for children who play the game, which involves strong violence, the solicitation of prostitutes to gain life points and then the murder of those prostitutes to gain one's money back. Parents who see actual clips from the game are generally discomforted and quite surprised at the themes, levels of violence and implications for attitudes toward women. Other games such as *Manhunt* are an order of magnitude more violent again.

Apart from often not knowing the content of many popular violent video games, many parents take false comfort from reports in the popular press that the 'jury is still out' regarding the impact of violent games on children's behaviour. Media reports often make much of the fact that there are a small number of violent video game studies that do not find an effect, and this seems to have led to a widespread belief that the scientific findings are inconclusive or are disputed by many researchers in the area. Contrary to popular belief, an overwhelming majority of violent video game studies *do* find an effect, and the better designed the studies are, the stronger the effect that they find (Anderson *et al.* 2010; Anderson and Warburton 2012). The latest review of studies by Craig Anderson and his colleagues in 2010 looked at over 380 studies that involved a staggering 130,000+ participants. Across the studies it was consistently found that playing violent compared with non-violent games:

- was causally linked with increases in aggressive behaviour in the short and long term

- was causally linked with desensitisation to violence in the short and long term

- was causally linked with increases in aggressive thoughts and feelings

- was causally linked with decreases in helping behaviour and empathy toward others.

Whenever there are several hundred studies of any social phenomenon, some will show no effect. This occurs in all scientific research. However, when it comes to violent video game effects, there are so many studies that do find an effect and so few that do not, that the vast majority of active and credible researchers in the area believe that the 'jury is no longer out' (Huesmann 2010; Krahé *et al.* 2012; Sacks *et al.* 2011; Warburton 2012a). The effects listed above have been shown in laboratory experiments, in real-world situations, in studies following people's behaviour across years in time and in studies of brain activity using brain imaging machinery. The sheer weight of the evidence is now very hard to ignore.

A final common fallacy believed by many parents (and promoted in the mass media) involves the idea that playing violent video games can help children to vent their aggression in a harmless environment, thus reducing the likelihood of aggressive behaviour in the real world (Baumeister, Heatherton and Tice 1994). The research in this area is quite clear. Behaving aggressively, whether on a sporting field, in everyday life, or when playing games, increases the likelihood of further aggression rather than reducing it (see Bushman 2002; Bushman, Baumeister and Stack 1999; Bushman, Baumeister and Phillips 2001; Geen, Stonner and Shope 1975). These studies suggest that playing violent games is very unlikely to reduce the likelihood of aggressive behaviour. Rather, Baumeister and colleagues (1994) suggest that the 'aggressive play vents aggression' argument is often is used as a justification for violent video game play, giving players permission to abandon their self-control and behave aggressively.

VIDEO GAMES AND GENDER

Interestingly, many studies show that the impacts of violent video games are similar for boys and girls. However, boys play so much more than girls that the 'dosage' is often much higher, and the impact correspondingly stronger. And this is the problem. The effect of violent video games increases when the violence in the game is stronger or bloodier and when the amount of exposure accumulates over the long term (Anderson *et al.* 2003; Barlett, Anderson and Swing 2009; Buckley and Anderson 2006). So, the more time that a child plays violent games, the more it becomes a 'risk factor', and the less time that the child is exposed to influences that may offset the risks (such as good parenting). For this reason, boys have more identified problems related to playing violent games than girls (for example, Gentile *et al.* 2011).

An interesting study that did find a gender difference was by Polman and colleagues in 2008. They wanted to see whether the interactive nature of video games increased their impact, and to this end had children either actively played or passively watched a video game. In this study the boys who played the violent video games were more aggressive immediately afterwards than those who simply watched the games. There was no such effect for the girls, suggesting that in this group, interactivity disproportionately affected the behaviour of boys.

Apart from interactivity, it is also possible that the type of game controller used by players may enhance the impact of playing violent video games on their thoughts, feelings and behaviours.

REALISTIC AND REPLICA WEAPON VIDEO GAME CONTROLLERS

A number of studies have examined the effects of realism in video games. For example, playing games in virtual reality environments has been shown to increase feelings of being immersed and involved in the game compared with standard game environments (Persky and Blascovich 2007), and games that are more advanced in terms of graphics and realism are also linked with increased immersion, involvement and physiological arousal (for example, Ivory and Kalyanaraman 2007). Also, it has been shown in a number of studies that using 'natural controllers' (such as the player being wired to a video game machine and the machine mapping his/ her body movements whilst using a tennis racquet) enhance both the enjoyment and the feeling of being immersed in the game (for example, McGloin, Farrar and Krcmar 2011; Skalski et al. 2011). Such controllers are also linked to better skills acquisition (for example, tennis skill in a tennis game). The probable reason is that such controllers, by using realistic props and movements, activate existing knowledge stored in the person's brain, leading to quicker mental processing and faster acquisition of skills and behaviour (see Gentile 2011; Tamborini and Skalski 2006). Other controllers require the user to learn game skills from scratch.

McGloin and colleagues (2011) suggest the same principles may extend to realistic controllers in violent video games. That is, using a replica gun in violent video games may facilitate faster learning of the skills and behaviours required, as well as facilitating increased immersion and involvement in the game. This is important, because, as Andre Melzer and his colleagues (2010) point out, immersion and involvement in a video game increases the degree to which players identify with the characters they play, and level of identification with an aggressive role model is a well-established factor in the learning of aggressive behaviour (see Huesmann et al. 2003). On theoretical grounds then, realistic weapon controllers may increase the impact of violent video games on aggressive behaviour. There are only a handful of studies that have tested this experimentally, but these have given interesting results.

Melzer and colleagues (2010) had students in Luxembourg play a violent video game with a standard mouse click controller versus a remote controller that allowed embodied gestures. Students using the remote controller 'tended to show more hostile cognitions' than those using the mouse click controller (p.171). Another study by Chris Barlett and colleagues (2007) in the US had participants play a shooter game with both a replica gun controller and a standard controller. Use of the replica gun resulted in comparatively higher hostility, physiological arousal and self-reported aggression. Markey and Scherer (2009) and Raney, Smith and Baker (2006) also note that gun-shaped controllers facilitate immersion into video games, thus strengthening the impact of the game on players.

Most recently, Jodi Whitaker and Brad Bushman (2012) had young adults play either a violent first-person shooting game or a non-violent, target-shooting game; some played with a standard controller and some with a replica gun controller. After playing their allotted video game, participants shot at a human-shaped target with a highly realistic replica gun containing 16 bullets. Compared with other groups, those who had shot at human targets with a replica gun had 99 per cent more headshots and were the only group to have more headshots than other shots. They also used 33 per cent more bullets than any other group. In the non-violent, target-shooting game, those who used the replica gun controller made more headshots than those using the standard controller. This study also examined the correlation between how many hours of shooting games were typically played by participants and behaviour in the study. Those who played more shooting games in real life fired more shots, fired more headshots and were more accurate at firing the realistic gun.

Although we clearly need more scientific evidence in this area, the studies to date suggest that replica weapon video game controllers (compared with standard controllers) probably facilitate greater learning of skills such as shooting ability, and are probably also linked with greater increases in the likelihood of aggression.

HOW DO VIOLENCE–RELATED ENTERTAINMENTS CAUSE CHANGES TO BEHAVIOUR?

We have already looked at the human tendency to imitate, but there are several well-known psychological processes that can explain why playing violent games or playing with weapon-themed toys might result in changes to the way children think, feel and behave. Most assume that the brain is made up of an 'associative neural network' of concepts in memory, and that the manner in which these concepts become linked together determines much of what we 'learn' to do. This may sound very technical, but really the concept is quite simple.

NEURAL NETWORKS

Human brains are 'wiring up' and changing every second of every day in response to what we experience, and they do so from well before birth right through to death. When people experience something new, clusters of neurons (long, thin nerve cells in the brain) are set aside to recognise that thing again. These clusters are called 'nodes', and humans have nodes for all sorts of objects, feelings and concepts. When we experience that thing again, the node becomes activated in recognition. Nodes that are activated together (because the two concepts the nodes represent are experienced together) become actually wired together in the brain, thus linking the two concepts (for example, the look of a rose and its smell). This wiring becomes stronger every time these two things are activated at the same time. This is a physical process that involves the forming of electrical and chemical pathways between neurons. The brain literally 'wires up' constantly in response to what is happening in our lives.

What is important for our purposes is that substantial amounts of information can be wired together into a 'knowledge structure' about a particular situation, such as what a supermarket is like, where the groceries are usually shelved and a 'script' for how you would normally behave there. In this example, when the concept of supermarket is activated by a trigger such as the supermarket logo, we know automatically what to do and don't need to think about it too much. We behave according to the script, almost on 'automatic pilot'.

This is an important concept in terms of aggressive behaviour because humans have lots of knowledge structures about situations where aggression might be used, especially if we have a lot of experience of those situations (for example, through living in a war-torn country, coming from a violent home or neighbourhood, or through experiencing violent virtual situations in the media or a video game). When a trigger from such an environment causes an aggression-related concept or knowledge structure to become activated in the brain, this increases the likelihood that an aggressive response will occur.

ACTIVATING AGGRESSIVE CONCEPTS IN THE BRAIN

A famous laboratory experiment by Berkowitz and LePage (1967) showed that the simple presence of a gun sitting on a table was enough to cause participants to give stronger electric shocks to other participants (that is, to be more aggressive). It was (and is) assumed that seeing the gun activated concepts related to guns in the memory of participants, who probably associated guns with aggressive behaviour and responded accordingly (Berkowitz 1970, 1974). This has been called the 'weapons effect'. Interestingly, the presence of an object not linked with aggressive behaviour (a badminton racquet) decreased aggressive behaviour, probably by activating non-aggressive concepts.

The weapons effect has been replicated many times since. For example, Craig Anderson and his colleagues showed in 1996 that simply viewing a weapon on a computer screen increased aggressive thoughts, and in 1998 that the viewing of weapon pictures (compared with non-weapon pictures) increased the ability of people to recall aggression-related words.

These findings have clear implications for replica weapon toys; how a child will behave during and after their use will probably depend on what concepts and scripts for behaviour are linked with those weapons in the child's mind. Because many children associate guns with killing and hurting and aggressive behaviour, it is reasonable to expect that the 'weapons effect' would also occur during play with replica weapons. This may explain why playing with replica guns has been linked with increases in aggressive behaviour.

This type of idea is central to other relevant theories as well. For example, according to the principles of 'script theory' (Huesmann 1986, 1998), toys can act as a trigger to retrieve from memory aggressive scripts for behaviour related to the toy (for example, if the toy is a weapon from a well-known cartoon series). Once activated, the script is rehearsed many times in fantasy play, and, as the aggressive behaviours are played out in more and more play situations, the script grows to include those behaviours in an ever-widening range of possible scenarios.

A related idea is 'cultural spillover' theory (Straus 1991), which suggests that the acceptance of violence in one sphere of life (such as in a video game or in play) legitimises it in other situations (such as interactions with family and friends).

EMOTIONAL DESENSITISATION TO VIOLENCE

When humans do something for any period, their emotional, cognitive and physiological response to it usually lessens over time (that is, they feel and think about that thing less, and their blood pressure and heart rate, etc. return to normal). Humans are not designed for prolonged arousal, and this process is one way – we are protected from over-stimulation and over-activation. However, such processes also mean that people become desensitised to aggressive media, violent games and presumably aggressive play (see Krahé et al. 2011). This is shown increasingly in brain imaging studies (for example, Montag et al. 2011; Strenziok et al. 2011), which demonstrate that emotional responding to violent media decreases in a relatively short period of time, and that people with a high level of prior exposure tend to have a smaller emotional response to violence they see (that is, they show long-term desensitisation). In addition, because such responses would normally trigger the process of morally assessing our experiences, desensitisation to violence may lead to the person not considering the moral implications of what they have seen, or of their own behavioural responses (Bushman and Anderson 2009). This in turn may lead to greater aggressive behaviour (Krahé et al. 2012).

SHOULD WE BE SURPRISED?

We have seen that boys imitate what they see, learn concepts and scripts for behaviour through the process of 're-wiring' the brain and will tend to behave in accordance with the thoughts and feelings that are most activated in the brain. In addition, they tend to become desensitised to violence with cumulative exposure. These processes underlie all social behaviours, not just aggression (Anderson *et al.* 2010), and it seems that similar principles apply to a range of violence-themed entertainments, including toys, video games and play. So, these effects should not surprise us. Indeed, multi-billion dollar industries are based on the assumption that such effects reliably occur, including the advertising industry, the toy and gaming industries and training programmes such as those for pilots and surgeons (Krahé *et al.* 2012).

SUMMARY AND SUGGESTIONS

Really, much of this is common sense. The things that boys are exposed to, including toys and games, impact on the way they think, feel and behave. This fits well with what we know about how people acquire knowledge and behaviours, and is backed up by research demonstrating that violence-themed entertainments for boys are linked with increases in aggressive behaviour, hostile thoughts and feelings, misogyny and a range of anti-social behaviours, as well as decreases in helping behaviours and desensitisation to the suffering of others (for example, Anderson *et al.* 2010; Warburton 2012a, 2012b).

Importantly, these effects are related to amount. Short-term effects are usually mild and short-lived (typically fading after 15–20 minutes or so). However, the effects are also cumulative (Buckley and Anderson 2006; Hasan *et al.* 2013). One piece of junk food does not cause a heart attack, one cigarette is highly unlikely to cause cancer, and playing one violent video game will probably not change boys greatly. However, prolonged exposure to entertainments with strongly violent themes is more likely to have a noticeable and enduring impact. This is good and bad news for those interested in healthy development. Smaller exposures are not usually problematic, but parents and professionals who work with children should be aware of the possible negative impacts of prolonged exposure.

One way that we can help boys with these issues is to help them think about toys, games and media in terms of healthy consumption, as we do with food. Children understand the basics of healthy eating, often from kindergarten, and should be able to understand that some types of play and toys are better in small quantities (like 'sometimes foods'), and that play thay encourages helping rather than unhelpful or hurting behaviours is a healthier play 'diet'. Like food, it boils down to moderation in terms of what and how much.

By taking this moderate approach and helping children to self-regulate and make their own good choices, we can encourage healthy play without being overly restrictive. Of course this is not easy, and not all responsibility can be put onto either the child or the parent. Regulators and policy makers should also take heed of the scientific evidence and play a responsible role in protecting boys from certain commercial practices where they can. Merchants and their advertisers have ensured that boys will be bombarded with messages designed to fuel their desire for all sorts of toys and entertainments (and especially those that are violence-themed), and so helping a boy to swim against the tide of peer pressure and commercial interests is never easy. It involves persistence, spending time playing with your child and, of course, being a good role model yourself.

ACKNOWLEDGEMENTS

I wish to thank Dr Ingrid Möller for reviewing this chapter, and Natasha Gupta, Claudia Nielson-Jones, Tamara Nothman and Ju-Hi Yi for their assistance with this chapter. Thanks very much to you all.

REFERENCES

Anderson, C.A. and Warburton, W.A. (2012) 'The Impact of Violent Video Games: An Overview.' In W.A. Warburton and D. Braunstein (eds) *Growing Up Fast and Furious: Reviewing the Impacts of Violent and Sexualised Media on Children*. Sydney: The Federation Press.

Anderson, C.A., Anderson, K.B. and Deuser, W.E. (1996) 'Examining an affective aggression framework: weapon and temperature effects on aggressive thoughts, affect and attitudes.' *Personality and Social Psychology Bulletin, 22*, 366–376.

Anderson, C.A., Benjamin, A.J. and Bartholow, B.D. (1998) 'Does the gun pull the trigger? Automatic priming effects of weapon pictures and weapon names.' *Psychological Science, 9*, 308–314.

Anderson, C.A., Berkowitz, L., Donnerstein, E., Huesmann, L.R. *et al.* (2003) 'The influence of media violence on youth.' *Psychological Science in the Public Interest, 4*, 81–110.

Anderson, C.A., Shibuya, A., Ihori, N., Swing, E.L. *et al.* (2010) 'Violent video game effects on aggression, empathy, and prosocial behavior in Eastern and Western countries.' *Psychological Bulletin, 136*, 151–173.

Anderson, C.A., Bartholow, B., Berkowitz, L., Brockmyer, J. *et al.* (2010) *Statement on Video Game Violence.* Professional testimony for the Gruel amicus curiae brief, *Arnold Schwarzenegger and Edmund Brown v Video Software Dealers Association and Entertainment Software Association,* Docket # 08-1448, Supreme Court of the United States.

Bandura, A. (1973) *Aggression: A Social Learning Analysis.* Englewood Cliffs, NJ: Prentice Hall.

Bandura, A., Ross, D. and Ross, S.A. (1961) 'Transmission of aggression through imitation of aggressive models.' *Journal of Abnormal and Social Psychology, 63*, 575–582.

Bandura, A., Ross, D. and Ross, S.A. (1963) 'Imitation of aggression through imitation of film-mediated aggressive models.' *Journal of Abnormal and Social Psychology, 66*, 3–11.

Barlett, C.P., Anderson, C.A. and Swing, E.L. (2009) 'Video game effects confirmed, suspected and speculative: a review of the evidence.' *Simulation and Gaming, 40*, 377–403.

Barlett, C.P., Harris, R.J. and Baldassaro, R. (2007) 'Longer you play, the more hostile you feel: examination of first person shooter video games and aggression during video game play.' *Aggression and Video Games, 33*, 1–12.

Baumeister, R.F., Heatherton, T.F. and Tice, D.M. (1994) *Losing Control: How and Why People Fail at Self-regulation.* San Diego, CA: Academic Press.

Benenson, J.F., Carder, H.P. and Geib-Cole, S.J. (2008) 'The development of boys' preferential pleasure in physical aggression.' *Aggressive Behaviour, 34*, 154–166.

Berkowitz, L. (1970) 'The contagion of violence: an S-R mediational analysis of some effects of observed aggression.' *Nebraska Symposium on Motivation, 18*, 95–135.

Berkowitz, L. (1974) 'Some determinants of impulsive aggression: the role of mediated associations with reinforcements for aggression.' *Psychological Review, 81*, 165–176.

Berkowitz, L. and LePage, A. (1967) 'Weapons as aggression-eliciting stimuli.' *Journal of Personality and Social Psychology, 7*, 202–207.

Blakemore, J.E.O. and Centers, R.E. (2005) 'Characteristics of boys and girls toys.' *Sex Roles, 53,* 619–633.

Buckley, K.E. and Anderson, C.A. (2006) 'A Theoretical Model of the Effects and Consequences of Playing Video Games.' In P. Vorderer and J. Bryant (eds) *Playing Video Games: Motives, Responses, and Consequences.* Mahwah, NJ: LEA.

Bushman, B.J. (2002) 'Does venting anger feed or extinguish the flame? Catharsis, rumination, distraction, anger, and aggressive responding.' *Personality and Social Psychology Bulletin, 28,* 724–731.

Bushman, B.J. and Anderson, C.A. (2009) 'Comfortably numb: desensitizing effects of violent media on helping others.' *Psychological Science, 20,* 273–277.

Bushman, B.J., Baumeister, R.F. and Phillips, C.M. (2001) 'Do people aggress to improve their mood? Catharsis beliefs, affect regulation opportunity, and aggressive responding.' *Journal of Personality and Social Psychology, 81,* 17–32.

Bushman, B.J., Baumeister, R.F. and Stack, A.D. (1999) 'Catharsis, aggression, and persuasive influence: Self-fulfilling or self-defeating prophecies?' *Journal of Personality and Social Psychology, 76,* 367–376.

Feshbach, S. (1956) 'The catharsis hypothesis and some consequences of interactions with aggressive and neutral play objects.' *Journal of Personality, 24,* 449–462.

Fletcher, R., St George, J. and Freeman, E. (2012) 'Rough and tumble play quality: theoretical foundations for a new measure of father–child interaction.' *Early Child Development and Care,* 1–14.

Geen, R.G., Stonner, D.M. and Shope, G.S. (1975) 'The facilitation of aggression by aggression: Evidence against the catharsis hypothesis.' *Journal of Personality and Social Psychology, 31,* 721–726.

Gentile, D.A. (2011) 'The multiple dimensions of video game effects.' *Child Development Perspectives, 5,* 75–81.

Gentile, D.A., Choo, H., Liau, A., Sim, T., Dongdong, L., Fung, D. and Khoo, A. (2011) 'Pathological video game use among youths: a two-year longitudinal study.' *Pediatrics, 127,* e319–e329.

Gonzales-Mena, J. (2008) *Foundations of Early Childhood Education.* Boston, MA: McGraw Hill.

Hasan, Y., Bègue, L., Scharkow, M. and Bushman, B. (2013) 'The more you play, the more aggressive you become: a long-term experimental study of cumulative violent video game effects on hostile expectations and aggressive behaviour.' *Journal of Experimental Social Psychology, 49,* 224–227.

Hellendoorn, J. and Harinck, H. (1997) 'War toy play and aggression in Dutch kindergarten children.' *Social Development, 3,* 340–354.

Huesmann, L.R. (1986) 'Psychological processes promoting the relation between exposure to media violence and aggressive behavior by the viewer.' *Journal of Social Issues, 42,* 125–140.

Huesmann, L.R. (1998) 'The Role of Social Information Processing and Cognitive Schema in the Acquisition and Maintenance of Habitual Aggressive Behavior.' In R.G. Geen and E. Donnerstein (eds) *Human Aggression: Theories, Research and Implications for Social Policy*. San Diego, CA: Academic Press.

Huesmann, L.R. (2010) 'Nailing the coffin shut on doubts that violent video games stimulate aggression: Comment on Anderson *et al.* (2010).' *Psychological Bulletin, 136*, 179–181.

Huesmann, L.R. and Kirwil, L. (2007) 'Why Observing Violence Increases the Risk of Violent Behavior in the Observer.' In D.J. Flannery, A.T. Vazsonyi and I.D. Waldman (eds) *The Cambridge Handbook of Violent Behavior and Aggression*. Cambridge: Cambridge University Press.

Huesmann, L.R., Moise-Titus, J., Podolski, C. and Eron, L. (2003) 'Longitudinal relations between children's exposure to TV violence and their aggressive and violent behavior on young adulthood.' *Developmental Psychology, 39*, 201–221.

Ivory, J.D. and Kalyanaraman, S. (2007) 'The effects of technological advancement and violent content in video games on players' feelings of presence, involvement, physiological arousal, and aggression.' *Journal of Communication, 57*, 532–555.

Jackman, G.A., Farah, M.M., Kellermann, A.L. and Simon, H.K. (2001) 'Seeing is believing: what do boys do when they find a real gun?' *Pediatrics, 107*, 1247–1250.

Klinesmith, J., Kasser, T. and McAndrew, F.T. (2006) 'Guns, testosterone, and aggression: an experimental test of a mediational hypothesis.' *Psychological Science, 17*, 568–572.

Klinger, L.J., Hamilton, J.A. and Cantrell, P.J. (2001) 'Children's perceptions of aggressive and gender-specific content in toy commercials.' *Social Behaviour and Personality, 29*, 11–20.

Krahé, B. and Möller, I. (2004) 'Playing violent electronic games, hostile attributional style, and aggression-related norms in German adolescents.' *Journal of Adolescence, 27*, 53–69.

Krahé, B., Möller, I., Huesmann, L.R., Kirwil, L., Felber, J. and Berger, A. (2011) 'Desensitization to media violence: links with habitual media violence exposure, aggressive cognitions, and aggressive behaviour.' *Journal of Personality and Social Psychology, 100*, 630–646.

Krahé, B., Berkowitz, L., Brockmeyer, J.H., Bushman, B.J. *et al.* (2012) 'Report of the Media Violence Commission.' *Aggressive Behavior, 38*, 335–341.

Lenhart, A., Kahne, J., Middaugh, E., Macgill, E.R., Evans, C. and Vitak, J. (2008) *Teens, Video Games, and Civics*. Washington, DC: Pew Internet and American Life Project.

Liss, M.B. (1981) 'Patterns of toy play: an analysis of sex differences.' *Sex Roles, 7*, 1143–1150.

McGloin, R., Farrar, K. and Krcmar, M. (2011) 'The impact of controller naturalness on spatial presence, gamer enjoyment, and perceived realism in a tennis simulation video game.' *Presence, 20*, 309–324.

Markey, P.M. and Scherer, K. (2009) 'An examination of psychoticism and motion capture ontrols as moderators of the effects of violent video games.' *Computers in Human Behavior, 25*, 407–411.

Melzer, A., Derks, I., Heydekorn, J. and Steffgen, G. (2010) 'Click or strike: realistic versus standard game controls in violent video games and their effects on aggression.' *Proceedings of the 9th International Conference on Entertainment Computing, 6243*, 171–182.

Mendoza, A. (1972) *The Effects of Exposure to Toys Conducive to Violence.* Unpublished doctoral dissertation. Miami, FL: University of Miami.

Montag, C., Weber, B., Trautner, P., Newport, B. *et al.* (2011) 'Does excessive play of violent first-person-shooter-video-games dampen brain activity in response to emotional stimuli?' *Biological Psychology, 89*, 107–111.

Owst, G.R. (1961) *Literature and Pulpit in Medieval England.* Oxford: Blackwell.

Persky, S. and Blascovich, J. (2007) 'Immersive virtual environments versus traditional platforms: effects of violent and non-violent video game play.' *Media Psychology, 10*, 135–156.

Polman, H., Orobio de Castro, B. and Aken, M. (2008) 'Experimental study of the differential effects of playing versus watching violent video games on children's aggressive behavior.' *Aggressive Behaviour, 34*, 256–264.

Potts, R., Huston, A.C. and Wright, J.C. (1986) 'The effects of television form and violent content on boys' attention and social behavior.' *Journal of Experimental Child Psychology, 41*, 1–17.

Raney, A.A., Smith, J.K. and Baker, K. (2006) 'Adolescents and the Appeal of Video Games.' In P. Vorderer and J. Bryant (eds) *Playing Video Games: Motives, Responses, and Consequences.* Mahwah, NJ: Lawrence Erlbaum.

Rideout, V.J. (2011) *Zero to Eight: Children's Media Use in America.* San Francisco, CA: Common Sense Media.

Rideout, V.J., Foehr, U.G. and Roberts, D.F. (2010) *Generation M2: Media in the Lives of 8–18 Year Olds.* Merlo Park, CA: Henry J. Kaiser Foundation.

Sacks, D.P., Bushman, B.J. and Anderson, C.A. (2011) 'Do violent video games harm children? Comparing the scientific amicus curiae "experts" in Brown v. Entertainment Merchants Association.' *Northwestern Law Review, 106*, 1–12.

Skalski, P., Tamborini, R., Shelton, A., Buncher, M. and Lindmark, P. (2011) 'Mapping the road to fun: natural video game controllers, presence, and game enjoyment.' *New Media and Society, 13*, 224–242.

Slife, B.D. and Rychlak, J.F. (1982) 'Role of affective assessment in modeling aggressive behaviour.' *Journal of Personality and Social Psychology, 43*, 861–868.

Straus, M. (1991) 'Discipline and deviance: physical punishment of children and other crime in childhood.' *Social Problems, 38*, 133–149.

Strenziok, M., Krueger, F., Deshpande, G., Lenroot, R.K., van der Meer, E. and Grafman, J. (2011) 'Fronto-parietal regulation of media violence exposure in adolescents: a multi-method study.' *Social Cognitive and Affective Neuroscience, 6*, 2–11.

Tamborini, R. and Skalski, P. (2006) 'The Role of Presence in Electronic Games.' In P. Vorderer and J. Bryant (eds) *Playing Video Games: Motives, Responses, and Consequences*. Maherah, NJ: Lawrence Erlbaum Associates.

Tanz, R., Christoffel, K.K. and Sagerman, S. (1985) 'Are toy guns too dangerous?' *Pediatrics, 75*, 265–268.

Turner, C.W. and Goldsmith, D. (1976) 'Effects of toy guns and airplanes on children's antisocial free play behavior.' *Journal of Experimental Child Psychology, 21*, 303–315.

Warburton, W.A. (2012a) 'Growing Up Fast and Furious in a Media Saturated World.' In W.A. Warburton and D. Braunstein (eds) *Growing Up Fast and Furious: Reviewing the Impacts of Violent and Sexualised Media on Children*. Sydney: The Federation Press.

Warburton, W.A. (2012b) 'How Does Listening to Eminem Do Me Any Harm? What the Research Says About Music and Anti-social Behaviour.' In W.A. Warburton and D. Braunstein (eds) *Growing Up Fast and Furious: Reviewing the Impacts of Violent and Sexualised Media on Children*. Sydney: The Federation Press.

Warburton, W.A. and Braunstein, D. (eds) (2012) *Growing Up Fast and Furious: Reviewing the Impact of Violent and Sexualised Media On Children*. Sydney: The Federation Press.

Warburton, W.A. and Highfield, K. (2012) 'Children, Media and Technology.' In J. Bowes, K. Hodge and R. Grace (eds) *Children, Families and Communities*. London: Oxford University Press.

Watson, M. and Peng, Y. (1992) 'The relation between toy gun play and children's aggressive behaviour.' *Early Education and Development, 3*, 370–389.

Whitaker, J.L. and Bushman, B.J. (2012) '"Boom, headshot!": Effect of video game play and controller type on firing aim and accuracy.' *Communication Research*, 30 April.

CHAPTER 5

CHANGING CHILDHOODS

NATURE DEFICIT

JAMES HAWES

During the last 50 years the world of childhood has undergone dramatic changes that create new challenges in how harm to children is considered, evaluated and regulated. In this chapter I examine the implications of the rapid increase of screen technology including children's mental, emotional and physical wellbeing. The 'hurry virus' (Honore 2004) is spreading a constant demand for faster broadband speeds, fast food and instant entertainment, yet the nation's children are at risk of becoming slower, unfit and sedentary, causing a whole range of emotional and physical disabilities (Moss 2012).

Paradoxically we live in a world where there is a rise in concern for the environment but the rapid decline in children spending actual time in it. Fifty years ago, 75 per cent of childhood was spent outside whereas now there is a shocking reversal of this percentage (Louv 2008). The outside is now seen as an incidental, dangerous or fearful place while the indoors has a greater allure. Richard Louv (2008) wrote the heavily researched book *Last Child in the Woods* and suggests that within the increasing disconnection from nature there is a large body of research indicating that an association with nature is good for our physical, mental and spiritual health. Stephen Moss (2012) concurs with Louv's findings from a UK perspective in the *Natural Childhood* report he wrote on behalf of the National Trust.

Around the globe governments have been busy introducing laws to protect children and maintain their rights while neglecting the dangers from media and commercial companies, allowing them child-free access (Marano 2012). This new internal threat creates grounds for a new understanding of significant harm, safeguarding and parental anxiety and confusion.

THE CAPTIVE CHILD

The technological and internet revolution has created a seismic shift in cultures, moving labour from physical and outdoor manufacturing work to sedentary, office-based work. When I was a boy, living in the country, nature was my playground. I played in my local environment and I roamed the local fields and rivers, building dens and imagining new and exciting adventures. At harvest I played in the fields, making forts and towers out of straw bales and playing with a wide range of peers. When I was a teenager, I helped on a farm; I drove tractors and went for trips on top of trailers stacked high with straw, ducking under trees and cables. In contrast, I recently arranged an outdoor campfire as part of my ten-year-old son's birthday. Some of the boys were clearly inexperienced in nature and were initially wary of the fire, but after a while they became totally engaged and enchanted by the sound, warmth, colour and engaging life outdoors. One boy commented, 'It's so much better then the fires on TV!' For the next two hours they happily whittled sticks, chatted, cooked bread, toasted marshmallows and watched the sparks and the night sky.

Within this sedentary and time-poor lifestyle, children are spending less time outside and when they are inside they are restricted. Louv (2008) cites James Clark (Professor of Kinesiology at University of Maryland) describing these children as 'containerised kids'. These children move from sitting in high chairs, to car seats and to buggies with very little active exercise. The same author cites an experiment on physical activity for three-year-olds by researchers at the University of Glasgow discovering that the toddlers in the sample were only active for 20 minutes a day. Below I highlight some of the key issues that have contributed to the captive child.

KEEP OFF THE GRASS

Louv (2008) believes that there has been a 'criminalisation' of natural play. Society has become impatient with the rowdiness and boisterousness of children outside and has been sending clear messages that children should be contained. Signs started to appear like 'Don't play on the grass', 'No ball games' and 'Climbing trees is prohibited' partly driven by health and safety concerns. Children have been left with the message that nature is dangerous – 'you can look but don't touch' – and dutifully play has retreated indoors. Unsurprisingly, this has resulted in commercial interests benefiting from indoor soft play centres where children are crammed into 'containers' to play under sanitised conditions. These centres prevent children from getting dirty and therefore parents can rest assured that the expensive branded clothing is preserved.

THE RISE OF CONTAINERISED PLAY

> The obesity epidemic coincides with the greatest increase in history of organised children's sport. (Louv 2008, p.48)

The majority of outdoor play is organised with rules and played within boundaries and lines under the supervision of adults and is generally competitive and combative in nature (Marano 2012). The false perception is that if more children are involved in some form of sport, it will be better for their health, but this has had little impact on preventing a growing obesity problem. In the process children lose freestyle play, which brings with it a whole range of skills from social regulation, creativity and health benefits. Commercially organised sport creates unique opportunities to sell products to children and young people, including 'junk' food and the latest kit.

LOSS OF WILD SPACES

Natural play spaces are disappearing with over-development, wild spaces in the country are being lost with the onset of industrialised farming and the green belt is being lost to the urban sprawl with the insatiable need to lay more concrete and build more buildings. Louv (2008) cites recent research by Robin Moore who has monitored the shrinkage and disappearance of urban wild spaces and also a study by Sandra Hofferth from the University of Maryland who measured a 50 per cent decline between 1997 and 2003 of children spending time in outdoor activities.

DANGER – GOING OUTSIDE IS FRIGHTENING!

The rise of exaggerated notions and media-influenced fear of the outside has contributed to the speed of indoor migration. The outdoor anxiety epidemic includes the dangers of traffic, outdoor accidents, stranger danger, child abduction, paedophilia and child abuse. However, statistically, as shown by several studies cited in Moss (2012), these dangers are unfounded: traffic deaths of children have actually fallen; being indoors is far more risky then being outdoors, with three times more children injured by falling out of bed then out of a tree. The same author cites other studies that reveal that 35,000 children a year are taken to A&E for falling down stairs. In terms of stranger danger and abuse the most dangerous place for children is their bedroom – most sexual abuse is carried out by family members.

INDUSTRIALISED EDUCATION

The education system has become a battleground of academic competition and intensive learning. This has contributed to education disappearing indoors where in the US 40,000 schools no longer have breaks and in the UK unstructured break times have been significantly reduced (Marano 2012). This industrialised schooling has been constructed via the fast education, influencing testing, lack of field trips and practical experiments, health and safety issues, litigation concerns and pure lack of time. Consequently, students who fail to contain themselves and disrupt the system lose unstructured outdoor breaks (Southall 2007).

There are many critics of the present educational system, including Fox (2006) who wonders if the educational system is causing trauma to students and teachers, with an epidemic in bullying, shaming, aggressive teaching, modern architecture and increasing competitive environments. Gray (2009) has no doubt that students believe that they are losing their freedom and that education is to be endured rather than pleasurable. Within my own work in newly built academies, several students have independently referred to the school architecture and structural system as a prison, complete with 'exercise yard' overlooked by the modern, class-clad corporate structure strewn with cameras. These students indicated that they perceive school as a kind of medicine, confinement or punishment, in which they are serving time and can't wait to be released!

Another student I work with succinctly described his experience of school by creating an acrostic for school: 'Six Crap Hours Of Our Life'. With these views it isn't difficult to understand why children are so disinterested in education. Furthermore, when students (usually boys) fail to fit into the system they are often excluded from the educational process or diagnosed with a medical disorder such as oppositional defiant disorder (ODD) or attention deficit hyperactive disorder (ADHD) (Southall 2007).

JUST WATCH IT!

A major contribution to the captive child and the migration indoors has been screen-based media (SBM). Children and young people have been born into a media-saturated world creating an 'always on' generation (Honore 2004). The pace of change during the last 20 years has been extraordinary, with screen technology morphing from television sets receiving terrestrial stations to 24/7 access of images, internet, video games, online gaming and the advent of portable devices. Many children now have entertainment hubs in their bedrooms, and with the development of wireless internet and portable devices, there has a been a large increase in consumption, with recent studies suggesting that children between the ages of 8 and 18 are exposed to an average of 7.5 hours of media a day (Monbiot 2012; Moss 2012).

DOES NATURE DISSOCIATION HARM CHILDREN AND YOUNG PEOPLE?

In what way does a dissociation of nature become a child protection issue and why should we be concerned? Louv (2008) observes that the DSM-IV (*Diagnostic and Statistical Manual of Mental Disorders*) (APA 2000) contains a disorder called 'separation anxiety disorder', an attachment-associated problem. He argues that a much more pervasive anxiety in present-day society is the disconnection from the natural world, and proposes an environmentally based definition of mental health. The migration indoors has been caused by the above issues and aided by the commercialisation of childhood and the medicalisation of children to quite frightening levels.

Southall (2007), a paediatrician based in Southampton, believes that society and pharmaceutical companies are pathologising children, ultimately suggesting that the children have been given a disorder because they don't fit into the new containers that society has created for them. Children's spheres have been reduced from the expanse of nature to the space of a modern house box, and society demands that they behave like mini adults.

LOSS OF CONNECTION WITH NATURE

The indoor migration shift has created dissociation with nature, where children and many adults are unable to identify common livestock, birds and trees (Moss 2012). They have lost contact with the origins of food and are almost shocked to think that the plastic-wrapped meat bought in shops and McDonald's once used to be a living, breathing animal. This became very real when I took a group of ten-year-old boys on a survival camp, which involved finding and cooking our own food. The boys found a rabbit being prepared for cooking disgusting and declared that they would not be partaking. The ones who were brave enough to eat it were surprised by its tastiness, suggesting it tasted like chicken!

LOSS OF CREATIVITY

The loss of unstructured play and outdoor learning is reducing children's opportunity for physical and emotional stretching, silence, imagination, exploratory play and creativity. When children are engaged in commercialised play, they lose the benefits of free-range play, including learning self-regulation, social interaction and increasing cognitive abilities (Marano 2012).

There is increasing evidence that reduction in a child's freedom correlates with a decline in their creativity. Peter Gray (2012) cites Kyung Hee Kim's three decades of research revealing a continuing decline in children's creativity. Evidence taken right across school ages marks that the decline began in the mid-1980s and continued. Kim says:

Children have become less emotionally expressive, less energetic, less talkative and verbally expressive, less humorous, less imaginative, less unconventional, less lively and passionate, less perceptive, less apt to connect seemingly irrelevant things, less synthesizing and less likely to see things from a different angle. (Kim 2011, quoted in Gray)

Children's lives are increasingly becoming over-structured by zealous hyper-parenting, educational monitoring and restrictive play, leaving less room for freedom, which reduces creativity potential. When children are deprived of time to roam, they fail to foster their imaginative potential, lose the ability to entertain themselves and feel bored (Gray 2012).

SLEEP DEPRIVATION

In my regular therapy work with teenagers, one of the common threads is tiredness, lack of sleep and sleep disturbance. This appears to be caused by a cocktail of delayed bedtime, bedroom entertainment suites, adrenalin-fuelled games, constant communication via texting and the intake of energy drinks. These young people are finding it difficult to turn off, shut down and relax. Recently I encountered the issue of sleep disturbance close to home when my ten-year-old son was finding it difficult to sleep. His friend had invited him to play *Call of Duty*, leaving him with frightening images.

ANXIETY AND DEPRESSION

Increasingly in my work with boys I have noticed what appears to be an anxiety epidemic that often goes unnoticed. The majority of boys who are referred to me with emotional, behavioural or anger problems are disguising emotions that boys find it socially unacceptable to express. These include any form of sadness, fear or shame that they feel unable to express. This emotional restriction may be one of the reasons why depression rates are rising fastest among children (Marano 2012).

THE ORIGINAL 'PLAY STATION' IS NATURE

As noted above, the nature of childhood is changing and it is affecting children's mental and physical health. Louv's (2008) comprehensive study into child's dissociation with nature and the negative results creates the term 'nature deficit disorder' (NDD) almost as an antidote to ADHD and other recently discovered mental disorders. Roszak (2001) challenges the dualistic nature of modern psychology in splitting the outer and the inner life and urges for a more holistic practice. He proposes the notion of 'ecopsychology', with a more integrated approach seeking to connect the urban psyche with an ecological consciousness. He proposes that healing can come from being more connected to the earth, its cycles and rhythms.

Louv (2008) is poignant about evidence and research into the benefits of nature when he says that few studies have been conducted because of the lack of commercial interest. Being in nature is free! However, the studies that have been conducted are generally via mental health charities and health services seeking to create lasting results and preventive measures.

Ecotherapy, a report from mental health charity Mind (2007), highlighted that GPs are prescribing antidepressants against their better judgement, because they feel there are no better alternatives. However, Mind's own research indicates that over 90 per cent of correspondents feel that green exercise is beneficial for their mental health. Basic mobility as against sedentary behaviour has a positive impact on how we feel, which could include activating endorphin and serotonin levels in the brain (Jackson 2012). Furthermore, researchers from the University of Glasgow found that exercise in green spaces provides more benefits than indoor exercise. Professor Rich Mitchell (2012) discovered that nature provides the brain with relaxing distractions, reducing levels of arousal. Nature allows a full sensual spectrum to be engaged and natural sounds in particular appear to help recovery.

I consume – therefore I am!

- 'I don't care if she isn't there as long as she buys me a new phone and buys all the things that I want… Mum, works to buy me things.'

- 'I can't live without my phone, I love my phone.'

- 'I got £500 cash for my birthday.'

These and other such sentiments about objects and money are some of the things that I regularly hear from the students, and yet within the same session they admit to desperately wanting positive attention from their parents.

> Whereas in previous generations their role in life was to contribute to the economy by working, now their role is to contribute by becoming consumers as early as possible. (Southall 2007, p.67)

Commercialisation has impacted on children's engagement with nature. In targeting youth and children, containerisation has been essential in creating commercial opportunities. When children are watching screens or involved in organised sports there is a potential to sell products and, paradoxically, junk food – London 2012 recently witnessed the creation of the biggest McDonald's in the world! Even magazines directed at children in favour of nature are packed with adverts for junk food, toys and films and characters that seek to dominate nature rather then enjoy being with it (Brown, Lamb and Tappen 2009).

PARENTS HAVE FORGOTTEN TO GROW UP!

What does parental and corporate responsibility mean today when considering the above issues? Alongside the nature of childhood changing, the nature of parenthood and ethical commercialism has changed. Parents and models of parenting have been impacted by the cult of 'more' (Honore 2004); they are addicted to small screens and super-size screens, stressed, time-poor and sedentary. Many family homes have dispensed with the table and television has become the new babysitter and is on 24/7; gadgets help to pacify and entertain the children, giving busy parents time to connect on social media sites or games. Family engagement and activity is minimal, with the majority of family time consisting of watching television or shopping (Southall 2007).

Is parenting style undergoing a radical change with the rise of blended and absent parenting, resulting in a loss of quality engagement? Many children have wrap-round childcare and are suffering from lack of attention and emotional contact. Increasingly 'pal-parenting' is the style of choice, where insecure adults refuse to create clear boundaries fearing upsetting their offspring and threatening their friendship. Additionally, 'hyper-attentive' or 'over-parenting' means that parents react to every difficultly in a child's day, eager to fix all their problems (Marano 2012). Alongside this, parents' anxiety about the above migratory effects has been replaced by a general indoor apathy resulting in a lack of monitoring and regulation concerning their screen behaviour. Many parents have yet to consider the emotional and possible physical risk that SBM causes, including early sexualisation, violence, solitary activity, lack of social skills and risking child development. (Braunstein, Plumb and Warburton 2012).

SAFEGUARDING CHILDREN FROM THE THREAT OF COMMERCIALISATION AND NATURE DEFICIT DISORDER

It is clearly not possible to stop the tsunami of SBM and the commercial gains that companies make from attracting children indoors without a fundamental shift in our value base. It also appears that in an age of austerity, environmental regulations are been scrapped, making it easier for wild spaces to disappear, schools, fields to be sold and brown sites to be recycled. However, if children are going to be protected and safeguarded, does governmental policy and regulation need to be stronger on advertising and violent media?

Ultimately there is evidence that media stereotyping of children is causing emotional restriction, trauma, over-sexualisation and a reliance on aggression. Creating a culture of 'more' is causing physical and psychological harm (Brown *et al.* 2009). Additionally, prescribing vast amounts of medication to children raises issues of safeguarding, where side effects are still relatively unknown and where free natural play could be the antidote (Louv 2008).

Furthermore, is it possible to stop the migration of children indoors? Is it possible to question the media's insistence that outdoors is dangerous? What is the role of media regulation and educational policy? Honore (2004) believes that we need to reinvent our whole philosophy of childhood to include freedom and fluidity, free-range play, reduced obsession with time and the need to mimic adults and empathise learning as a joy (Fox 2006). The loss of freestyle outdoor play is impacting the physical and psychological wellbeing of children, and as such it does raise questions outlined by Jim Wild in the introduction to this book – how can child protection become broader?

REFERENCES

APA (American Psychiatric Association) (2012) *Diagnostic and Statistical Manual of Mental Disorders IV.* Arlington, VA: APA.

Braunstein, D., Plumb, J. and Warburton, W. (2012) 'Media and Social Policy: Towards an Evidence Based Approach to Content Regulation in a Media Saturated World.' In W. Warburton and D. Braunstein (eds) *Growing Up Fast and Furious: Reviewing the Impacts of Violent and Sexualised Media on Children.* Adelaide: The Federation Press.

Brown, L.M., Lamb, S. and Tappen, E.D. (2009) *Packaging Boyhood: Saving Our Sons from Superheroes, Slackers and Other Media Stereotypes.* New York: St Martin's Press.

Fox, M. (2006) *The A.W.E. Project: Reinventing Education, Reinventing the Human.* Kelowna, BC: Copperhouse.

Gray, P. (2009) 'Why don't students like school? Well, duhhh… Children don't like school because they love freedom.' *Psychology Today.* Available at: www.psychologytoday.com/blog/freedom-learn/200909/why-don-t-students-school-well-duhhh, accessed on 28 April 2013.

Gray, P. (2012) 'As children's freedom has declined, so has their creativity.' *Psychology Today.* Available at: www.alternative-learning.org/?p=888, accessed on 28 April 2013.

Honore, C. (2004) *In Praise of Slow: How a Worldwide Movement is Challenging the Cult of Speed.* London: Orion.

Jackson, C. (2012) 'The joy of exercise.' Therapy Today, 23, 6. Available at www.therapytoday.net/article/show/3198, accessed on 20 May 2013.

Kim, K.H. (2011) 'The creativity crisis: the decrease in creative thinking scores on the Torrence Tests of Creative Thinking.' *Creative Research Journal, 23,* 285–295. In P. Gray (2012) 'As children's freedom has declined, so has their creativity.' *Psychology Today.* Available at: www.alternative-learning.org/?p=888, accessed on 28 April 2013.

Louv, R. (2008) *Last Child in the Woods – Saving Our Children from Nature Deficit Disorder.* New York: Algonquin Paperbacks.

Marano, H.E. (2012) 'A nation of wimps.' *Psychology Today.* Available at www.psychologytoday.com/articles/200411/nation-wimps, accessed on 28 April 2013.

Mind (2007) *Ecotherapy: The Green Agenda for Mental Health.* London: Mind.

Mitchell, R. (2012) 'Is physical activity in natural environments better for mental health than physical activity in other environments?' *Social Science & Medicine.* Cited in C. Jackson, 'The joy of exercise.' *Therapy Today,* 23, 6.

Monbiot, G. (2012) 'Housebroken: there's a second environmental crisis, just as potent as the first.' *The Guardian,* November.

Moss, S. (2012) *Natural Childhood.* Swindon: National Trust. Available at www.nationaltrust.org.uk/document-1355766991839, accessed on 4 November 2012.

Roszak, T. (2001) *The Voice of the Earth: An Explanation of Ecopsychology* (2nd edition). Grand Rapids, MI: Phannes Press.

Southall, A. (2007) *The Other Side of ADHD: Attention Deficit Hyperacticity Disorder Exposed and Explained.* Oxford: Radcliffe Publishing.

CHAPTER 6

THE MYTH OF CHOICE FOR CHILDREN AND PARENTS

WHY WE DENY THE HARM BEING CAUSED TO OUR CHILDREN

RENATA SALECL

How are children and young people to manage their emotions and aspirations in a world so engulfed by the magic of consumerism and the internalized notion that anything and everything is possible?

From early childhood on, young people are deeply affected by advertising as well as by the ideology that convinces them that they can make out of their lives what they want and that everyone can make it in today's world. They are also under the impression that they can make idea choices in their lives and that happiness and self-fulfilment are what their lives are supposed to be about.

Sadly, the ideology of choice which stresses the power of the individual has contributed to new forms of suffering that young people experience today. From early psychoanalytic writings we know that malaise of civilization and malaise of the individual go hand in hand. Social changes thus affect the symptoms of malaise people suffer from and the new symptoms people develop, of course, affect society as a whole (Freud 1930).

In the last decade, there have been many contemporary debates about how social changes that we experience in postindustrial capitalism affect individuals. The ideology of postindustrial capitalism has heavily relied on the idea of choice, freedom, self-determination and endless progress.[1] The underside of this ideology, however, has been an increase in anxiety, in the individual's feelings of inadequacy, and guilt for not making it in today's world.[2] Until very recently, the ideology of choice has actually functioned very well to prevent any questioning about possible social change. The individual was rather engaged in constant self-change—often to the point of self-destruction.

French psychoanalyst, Jacques Lacan, pointed out that the idea of self-destruction is very much aligned with how capitalism functions. In recent years there has been growing interest in his thesis that he developed in the early seventies at a lecture in Milan that capitalism elevated the subject into the position of the master who no longer considers him or herself as a proletarian slave, but identifies with the ideology of endless possibilities, up to the point of considering everything in his or her life as a matter of choice.[3] On top of this, the society in which children and young people are now living is speeding up. Middle-class children today are often overwhelmed by activities they need to engage in after school, while they are also encouraged to take extra lessons for the best results in various placement tests that will open up their best chances for university education.

Children as well as their parents, however, not only work longer hours and consume more and more, they also, at some point, in a paradoxical way, start consuming themselves. Workaholism, addiction, anorexia, bulimia and self-cutting thus become symptoms people suffer from in the developed world. Slowly these symptoms push them onto various paths of self-destruction. The paradox, however, is that people seem to be oblivious to what is happening to them and continue believing in the ideology of endless possibilities—this is the lifestyle they are also bequeathing to their children who not surprisingly often feel entitled to enjoy the lifestyle they associate with enjoyment and success.

Identification with the ideology of choice has not only contributed to the formation of new psychological symptoms where people impose particular new forms of aggression toward themselves, it has also encouraged various forms of social violence

---

1   I develop this point further in *The Tyranny of Choice* (Salecl 2011).
2   More on anxiety in post-industrial capitalism in *On Anxiety* (Salecl 2004).
3   This lecture is unpublished. The main points that Lacan developed there have been analyzed in *Lebrun* (2009).

through which the youth are showing their rage at society at large which, in the midst of an ideology of endless possibilities, actually more and more limits the youth to make it in today's world.

SELF-DESTRUCTION AND THE PROBLEM WITH ONE'S IMAGE

What do children and young people really see when they are looking at themselves in the mirror and are often dissatisfied with their appearance? We know that observing oneself in the mirror has never been easy. From Greek mythology we know the story of Narcissus, whose fascination with the reflection of his own image ultimately cost him his life. While Narcissus could not stop observing his reflection, today the problem is more the inability of people to observe themselves in the mirror. Those who suffer from anorexia, for example, are often horrified by seeing themselves as very fat in the mirror while in reality they might be dangerously thin.

Japanese psychoanalyst Daisuke Fukuda has noticed a very special relationship with the mirror, held by some Japanese girls at a time when Japanese culture has become overwhelmingly obsessed with ideas of beauty and when young people have become more and more burdened with the image of an ideal body.[4] One Japanese student, for example, sought psychoanalytic help because she had the urge to break every mirror that appeared in her vicinity. This girl not only avoided looking at herself in the mirror, but also actively engaged in ruining surfaces in which she could see her reflection.

The occurrence of such a painful symptom is in a particular way linked to the changes that are happening in Japan in regard to people's perception of their image. In recent years Japan has experienced a significant growth in the beauty industry. In many public places, Japanese girls are now flooded with free newspapers offering a complete change in their appearance. At first glance, these newspapers look like the usual fashion magazines, but they are full of advertising for surgical procedures with various special offers and coupons for special discounts. Thus one's appearance more and more looks like a consumer object that one simply buys. Until recently, Japanese culture reflected the view that people

---

4   Private conversation with author.

need to accept their appearances. Now one's body is perceived as a matter of choice.

The emergence of new psychological symptoms, of course, cannot be taken as something that directly reflects the changes in ideology. Thus we cannot say that Japanese girls are now breaking the mirrors or universally trying to change their bodies. Individuals always form symptoms in very individualized ways.

From our early childhood, however, the way we see ourselves in the mirror is influenced by others around us and by culture in general (see Lacan 2002). When the baby goes through the mirror stage, it is essential that he or she identify his or her image via the speech of the primal caregiver (see Lacan 2004). It is usually the mother who urges the baby to recognize him or herself in the mirror.

The authority figures around us (our parents) and society in general also soon start acting as particular mirrors in which we start observing ourselves. When social perceptions about body change, we also start regarding ourselves in different ways. Susie Orbach, in her book *Bodies*, shows how we perceive nakedness, weight, and beauty differently if we live in different cultural settings (Orbach 2009). However, she also points out that these settings can mark us in an unconscious way, which is why a person who in his or her early childhood has been brought up with a particular attitude toward the body might have difficulty changing when he or she starts living in a different social context.

While some people can be deeply marked by the cultural imprints they received in their early childhood, others might be more susceptible to cultural changes that happen during their life span. To this point, Orbach mentions the case of Papua New Guinea, which in the past perceived as an ideal of beauty a rather shapely female body (Orbach 2009). With the advent of the international media, however, this ideal quickly changed, and in a couple of years this country, too, started experiencing a large increase in anorexia and bulimia.

If today we often have the impression that we can alter the way we see reality or ourselves to conform to the way that we wish, this freedom paradoxically has also opened doors to new forms of ignorance; thus, it often looks that in the midst of all these possibilities to alter our perceptions, we choose rather to turn a blind eye and opt for not seeing at all. Why is it that in the midst of presumably endless possibilities people opt for ignorance, especially in regard to the fact that their possibilities are actually much more limited than they think they are?

THE PASSION FOR IGNORANCE

When societies experience radical changes, we can also observe a change in the way people (particularly children and young people) start looking at themselves. It is as if the mirror in which they have been observing themselves has changed, and as a result people start looking at themselves in a different way. Let us take the case of authorities. If we perceive authorities as a particular type of a mirror that we look into on a daily basis—try to identify with them, oppose them, or search for recognition from them—we can observe a change happening when society itself gives authorities a different role. When, for example, the ideology encourages us to stop looking at authorities and rather take ourselves as the ultimate master, we might become indifferent toward what others think about us and to how our behavior affects others.

This ignorance toward others and toward society at large is today shifting to ignorance toward oneself. Contemporary narcissism thus seems in a particular way to predicate auto-destructive behavior in children and young people. It is not that the individual is primarily centered on his or her well-being. Paradoxically, in the midst of all the information that people today have, the individual often turns away when something seems too traumatic.

In order to understand the nature of this ignorance, it is necessary to distinguish between ignorance and repression. When we find something very traumatic, repression usually helps to (at least temporarily) establish some distance from what is for us too painful or frightening. An example might be a young person who experienced a traumatic violent event in early childhood, but later has no memory of it. When it comes to ignorance, however, we deny that something is traumatic. A person behaves as if the latter does not concern him or her. It is almost as if we have a foreclosure at work where the subject is not marked by language. An individual thus can have all the information on the threat or rejection, but will behave as if nothing had happened. This kind of ignorance, paradoxically, can contribute to an illusionary feeling of all powerfulness.

The passion for ignorance is now appearing on a variety of levels. In spite of the continuing economic crisis, most countries are behaving as if it is just a bad dream from which they will eventually wake up and then everything will be as usual. With the ongoing ecological problems that are becoming more and more alarming, we are behaving as if nothing really has to change. Indeed, as children and young people grow into the world, what methods of repression come into play when they are faced with startling information about climate change or witness for themselves some visceral sense that all is not well with the environment as they see their own localized weather patterns disrupted and prone to volatility? What is the cost to their psychological health to ignore or deflect their fears about the future?

Until very recently, we also had passion for ignorance in regard to raising social inequality in the developed world. The success of the ideology of late capitalism has been that it created the fantasy of possibility even in the midst of obvious impossibilities. Even the very poor who have fewer and fewer choices would passionately support the idea of choice.

Louis Althusser pointed out that ideology functions in such a way that it creates a veil of obviousness (Althusser 1971). This operation has been very strong in recent years since questioning where capitalism is going and whether there is an alternative to the organization of society as we know it has been almost nonexistent in the public sphere.

How did this passion for ignorance manifest itself? Dan Ariely and Michael Norton conducted a study on how people perceive social inequality (Norton and Ariely 2011). They asked participants of a survey how much of the US wealth is in the hands of the richest 20 percent of people, and what would be a just distribution of wealth. People guessed that the richest 20 percent probably have about 60 percent of all of the wealth, but that the just distribution would be for them to have about 30 percent. In reality, however, the top 20 percent have more than 80 percent of the wealth.

Why do people not rebel against what they actually perceive as an unjust distribution of wealth? Why do they not, for example, more enthusiastically support larger taxes on the rich and universal health care? When presenting the results of the Norton and Ariely study, *The New York Times* asked different commentators to explain the lack of people's reactions against wealth inequality, especially since the majority of people imagine that in an ideal world the inequality would be much smaller than it is (Norton *et al.* 2011). While some commentators pointed out that people still have so-called "lottery mentality" and think that they might make it in the future, others stressed that many do not actually believe that they will succeed; however, they imagine that their children might. Which is why these people often do not support the idea of taxing the rich—since they imagine that their son might become a new Bill Gates, they do not want to punish him with higher taxes. These people are often in denial about the possibilities their children will have in life—especially if they are part of the lower classes.

Denial, however, is also part of today's consumerism. The ideology that encourages us to believe that everyone can make it in today's society opens up the perception that everyone can also consume in an equal way. Thus, it is not surprising that some of the riots that we have witnessed in the last few years had a particular consumerist mark.

PAINFUL PASSION FOR LUXURY

Looking at the faces of the children and young people who engaged in the London riots, which were later put on the internet by the British police, we can say that many of the rioters experienced at least temporary satisfaction from looting the shops. Theorists who have analyzed the issue of happiness in the last decade could have easily observed that happiness can be at least temporarily increased by the act of looting. The signs of obvious pleasure were everywhere on the faces of the young looters in London that were presented in the media. One young woman who clutched in her hands a bunch of shoes looked as if she was experiencing a special mystical enjoyment. A young man running with a stack of jeans was caught by the camera, giggling happily. Another one who was carrying a bunch of sportswear also looked as if he was in an elated state.

In collective violence, there is often a pleasure that participants experience in transgressing social norms. The fact that someone is part of a group often reduces anxiety and guilt, and gives the illusion of security. The feeling of elation that participants in the acts of violence experience is visible in many social rituals.

Violence has in the last few years also been glorified in corporations and large financial institutions. The fact that we have to destroy competition, ruthlessly search for profit, and take the scalps of our competitors has been a constant theme for some time in the business discourse. Psychological analysis of top players in this world has also shown the lack of feelings of guilt and the lack of concern for others (see Babiak and Hare 2006). A businessman once explained to me that negotiations are most easily completed if he throws something on the floor or makes an unexpected aggressive gesture in another way. Ironically, the behavior of rioters on the streets of London is not so different from those who are running the corporations that they looted, only that they expressed violence in a public sphere and they have been subject to criminal sanctions.

The London riots have also shown another similarity between the higher and lower classes—their almost religious love of luxury. During these riots, a casual observer recorded and forwarded to the media the conversation of some girls who were deciding what to steal from the shops that were broken into. One of the girls asked the other whether they should steal cosmetics from Boots (a non-expensive drug store); the girl, however, responded that it would be much better to loot The Body Shop since it had more expensive products. This example shows how much even the poorest people show a desire for luxury items and how effective advertising has been in recent years.

Advertising often presents to children and young people desired consumer objects with the help of the idea of transgression. Here the sellers of sports goods and casual fashion clothes have been at the forefront of creating important points of identification among the poor youth. Thus, it is not surprising that among the most looted shops in the UK were those belonging to the sportswear chain JD Sports (see *The Guardian* and London School of Economics and Political Science 2011). In recent years, JD Sports has invested heavily in a marketing campaign to become one of the most desired brands among British youth. An exceptional marketing success came when the company began propagating "Gangster chic" and "danger wear" images. Many well-known brands were thus effectively promoting the idea that the consumer of their products was someone who went against the regime. During the riots, the well-known retailer of denim, Levi's, withdrew its new advertising poster, which showed the back of a young, aggressive man dressed in Levi's walking toward a large group of police who were looking as if they were prepared for an attack. Underneath this image was written "Go forth!" (Newton 2011).

At the time of the riots, one of the most worried companies was Adidas, since a large number of rioters were dressed from head to toe in Adidas clothes. Adidas in the last few years has become famous for using well-known rappers in their advertising who have had problems with the law. Not surprisingly, many young people who were looting the stores in London looked very much like the images of the rebels featured in recent advertising campaigns.[5]

What we experience as a luxury item or a luxury experience has changed throughout history. Luxury, however, has always been in some way linked to transgression. To perceive something as a luxury, this object as an experience has to be in some way inaccessible, expensive, prohibited, or otherwise hard to get. And for one person having a desire to possess it or experience it, it is necessary that other people want it, too. James B. Twitchell, in his book on the history of luxury, points out that the first public examples of luxury were church relics (Twitchell 2002). In the Middle Ages, when churches wanted to possess some relic, they had to steal it from another church. And later, luxury was heavily tied to theft. The history of wars, for example, is also the history of thefts of what was at some point perceived as an element of luxury.[6]

The perception of luxury has changed radically over the last few decades. In the past, luxury items were often associated with good quality and durability. Now, with mass production, the quality of the object has become unimportant. Now one only buys the name—a brand—and the object can easily be made poorly. The idea that the object can easily be discarded and replaced by another one has replaced the previous perception that the object's sublime quality relied on its durability.

We started comparing brands with a lifestyle, while at the same time we also experienced some kind of democratization of luxury. In the past, there existed a hierarchy of how people acquired luxury. First the rich became fascinated by particular luxury objects, later

---

5   The paradox of the London riots, however, is that large firms like Adidas quickly tried to figure out how to disassociate themselves from the rioters who were wearing their clothes, while other lesser known fashion firms were delighted with newspaper images of a rioter wearing their products. They took this as free advertising, which they were happy to get.

6   An account of the history of art theft at the time of the Second Word War is provided in Nicholas 1994.

the middle classes followed, and in the end the lower classes got the chance to experience cheaper versions of those objects. A major turning point occurred when the brands started producing a range of less expensive items that were made immediately available to the lower classes. Today, if someone cannot afford a Prada dress, he or she can buy a Prada wallet or, of course, purchase a counterfeited version. The important thing is no longer possession of an object, but identification with what this object represents—which is why the object can be fake, but the sublime quality related to its brand name can still function.

The ideology of postindustrial capitalism, which addresses the individual as someone who has endless possibilities to create a life that he or she wants and endlessly go from one "cool" object to another, contributed to people deciding to acquire those objects with acts of violence. Ironically, on the one hand, capitalism today advertises unlimited growth in profits and limitless consumption, but on the other hand, it seems to require an extreme version of self-restraint from those who have nothing. While those who have nothing are constantly bombarded with new luxury items, they seem to only be allowed to look at them from afar—or sometimes touch them in new experience type of shops (like the famous Apple Store where people can endlessly play with new gadgets), but not take them to their poor homes.

Until recently, the success of ideology of choice has been that it has, on the one hand, portrayed choice as primarily an individual matter and, on the other hand, has created a perception that by making the right choices one can overcome social disadvantages. This ideology has also heavily relied on people's feelings of guilt and inadequacy for not making it. The turn toward self-critique, self-destruction, and self-restraint in regard to abundance of consumer goods has prevented people from engaging in social critique and from attempting to think about choice as social choice—as a mechanism that can bring about social change. However, for the social critique to be effective, it is necessary to reinterpret the idea of choice and to open up space to new visions about how society in the future needs to be organized.

The legacy we are passing on to our youth should thus go less in the direction of presenting the ideas of choice in terms of individual consumer choices, and rather as an opening to envision different forms of social organization that they might inhabit in the future.

REFERENCES

Althusser, L. (1971) *Lenin and Philosophy, and Other Essays.* London: New Left Books.

Babiak, P. and Hare, R.D. (2006) *Snakes in Suits: When Psychopaths Go to Work.* New York: HarperCollins.

Freud, S. (1930) *Civilization and its Discontents.* London: Leonard & Virginia Woolf. Authorized Translation by Joan Riviere. Ann Arbor, MI: University of Michigan Library.

Guardian, The and London School of Economics and Political Science (2011) *Reading the Riots: Investigating England's Summer of Disorder.* Available at www.guardian.co.uk/uk/interactive/2011/dec/14/reading-the-riots-investigating-england-s-summer-of-disorder-full-report, accessed on 28 April 2013.

Lacan, J. (2002) *Écrits: A Selection.* New York and London: W.W. Norton & Co.

Lacan, J. (2004) *Le Séminaire de Jacques Lacan. Livre X, L'Angoisse, 1962–1963.* Paris: Seuil.

Lebrun, J.-P. (2009) *Un Monde Sans Limite: Suivi de Malaise dans la Subjectivation.* Ramonville Saint-Agne: Éd. Erès.

Newton, M. (2011) 'Levi's Latest "Go Forth" Ad Romanticizes Youth Riots at the Wrong Time.' Available at www.forbes.com/sites/matthewnewton/2011/08/10/levis-latest-go-forth-ad-romanticizes-youth-riots-at-the-wrong-time, accessed on 28 April 2013.

Nicholas, L.H. (1994) *The Rape of Europa: The Fate of Europe's Treasures in the Third Reich and the Second World War.* New York: Knopf.

Norton, M.I. and Ariely, D. (2011) 'Building a better America: one wealth quintile at a time.' *Perspectives on Psychological Science, 9,* 10.

Norton, M.I., Cowen, T., Freeland, C. and Winship, S. (2011) 'Rising wealth inequality: should we care?' Room for Debate. *The New York Times,* 21 March. Available at www.nytimes.com/roomfordebate/2011/03/21/rising-wealth-inequality-should-we-care?hp, accessed on 20 May 2013.

Orbach, S. (2009) *Bodies.* London: Profile Books.

Salecl, R. (2004) *On Anxiety.* London and New York: Routledge.

Salecl, R. (2011) *The Tyranny of Choice.* London: Profile Books.

Twitchell, J.B. (2002) *Living It Up: Our Love Affair with Luxury.* New York: Simon & Schuster.

PART 2

SEXUAL EXPLOITATION

CHAPTER 7

THE COMMERCIALISATION OF GIRLS' BODIES

SUSIE ORBACH

Whatever children are exposed to, they have to find a way to manage. They absorb, reject, transform and imagine on the basis of experience or fragments of experience.

In this context, consumerism isn't something outside of children's experience that happens to them or is slowly introduced. There isn't a clean consumption-free space that gradually changes so that at some point children get to know about ways of being. The world children are introduced into is busy, busy, busy with things and with screens and moving images. If you look at the TV, the programming for babies and children represents a background activity – what the media people call wallpaper. There isn't a background of quiet. While it is not that demanding, it nevertheless colonises the environment of the baby and the carers and in so doing creates a particular kind of world. Consumerism has come to constitute who we are and it is thus embedded in who we are, in our relation to self and how we communicate.

THERE IS NO SUCH THING AS A PURE SPACE

The mother–child relationship is the most important relationship in a child's life. Despite many men's involvement with their children or the fact that there are people who jointly raise their children and gay male couples raising children, I think it is still the case that predominantly, the mother (or a female substitute) is the primary parent.

If we turn now to the mother–daughter relationship, a daughter's first love affair is with her mother. That relationship welcomes the infant into the world and it is the model for all relationships. It is like an emotional imprint. How a mother relates to her baby girl or baby boy of course will be a model; it will form a template for relationships in the future (see Eichenbaum and Orbach 1982).

How a mother relates to her baby's body and her own body will become the template for how that infant, then toddler, then little girl/little boy relate to their own body. In pre- and post-partum clinics you can hear anxiety about the body and anxiety about body size. Part of what is occurring now, in these time of troubled bodies where women's bodies are continually under assault, is that a mother comes to relate to her own body in ways that can be hypercritical and preoccupied.

Huge industries spend extraordinary amounts of money destabilising women's bodies and in very effective ways so that women then come to have disturbed relationships with their bodies, feeling that they are not alright, and that they should constantly be fixing, worrying, improving, assessing, exercising, restraining, enhancing and disciplining their bodies. This has created a situation in which a body is increasingly felt to be unsafe. It is not a treasured or even an ordinary place to live from but a project that requires continual work (Orbach 2009).

This often means that insecurity around food and the body are not choices or incomprehensible outcomes, they are actually predictable outcomes at this point. We can predict the level of eating difficulties; we have already seen it from this generation of girls who are very, very disturbed in their bodies because their mothers were disturbed.

These observations are not intended to blame the mothers at all. I hope you understand that; I think that you probably will. Children mimic the familial environment around food. If the parent fusses about what their child eats – and it is hard not to this day and age – and as well is fussing about her own food and intake, there is a double fussing going on. It is not just an anxiety about what the child is eating. Eating becomes fraught or an arena for conflict. Bodies and eating are no longer straightforward; there is so much anxiety that eating problems and body image problems start horrifyingly early and abound.

Let's take a particular example that is increasingly occurring; young women's use of botox. A baby's intelligence – its emotional intellectual intelligence – develops through reading faces. Faces that move, faces that frown, faces that smile, faces where the noses wrinkle up, faces where you can follow the other, faces where questions can be read, faces where joy can be reflected and faces where sadness can be seen are crucial for psychological development (Orbach 2011). For a baby to absorb the facial expressions that are a mirror to their own emotional life so that they actually internalise the whole gamut of emotional ranges, they need to have mobile faces that show and reflect different feelings and different energies to play with. There is concern now amongst infant researchers looking at how babies develop that when botox is injected around the eyes and smile lines, the capacity of the adult to convey the subtlety of feeling is diminished.

It is quite a serious development because instead of an infant experiencing curiosity and liveliness in the face, there is a certain blankness. If you look at Professor Tronic's tapes (YouTube 2013), the child psychiatrist in Boston who is Director of the Child Development Unit at Harvard University, you can see what happens when a mother presents a blank face. In the space of a minute that child has gone from an ordinary aliveness to being depressed and withdrawn. It tries everything to engage and interact with the mother. Tronic does this intentionally to make a developmental point, but if we now apply this phenomenon to a mother's face that is constrained by botox we can see similar results. Such problems are not unknown to film directors, who are unable to do close ups with their actors unless they edit in some lines and wrinkles.

Mothers are encouraged to have botox as one of the by-products of the commercialisation of the body. If we now turn to children, we see the intense commercialisation of the child in its particularly gendered form in which girls and femininity are represented as always including beautification; the way that girls are invited to belong is through taking up these very limited images of femininity.

Many of the images of children are highly sexualised at the same time as being extremely cute, but the saturation of pornified images is now limiting the ways in which children and especially girls' imagination can develop. It is not that children aren't sexual – I think we do know, since Freud, that childhood sexual desire exists – but that isn't the same as saying that children need to be already perceiving of themselves as being represented in sexual poses all of the time. If imagination is only encoded in princesses and sexual terms for girls – the 'Disneyfication' if you like of life – then the space for other inventive possibilities is limited, not just for those girls but for the boys that they meet and culture in general.

It isn't much better for boys. I think it is equally abusive to represent masculinity in terms that suggest that the point of life is to kill. Feminism fought very hard to illuminate the gendered arrangements in which girls were brought up to be carers and boys to be providers of economic security. That emotional–economic arrangement (Orbach and Eichenbaum 1984) prevailed alongside the heroic job of going to war. Boys used to be raised to be killers. It is only recently in the West that they haven't been uniformly. If a boy's emotional life is constrained in these ways, it is similarly limiting.

If we turn to look at the TV show *Toddlers in Tiaras* we find real evidence of abuse. It is possible to look at it as a freak show but if we slow down and see what is going on we can notice that it takes place in community buildings in various North American, often working-class, communities. We observe girls as young as four being put through routines to make them sexually alluring puppets. We can observe highly elaborate hair treatments, botox, spray tan and nails, mini stripper outfits and the coaching of pole dancing routines.

At the other end of the market in class terms it is disturbing to view last summer's French *Vogue* with its 17 pages of paedophilic images showing ten-year-old model, Thylane Blondeau (Daily Mail 2011). There are many arguments about whether or not she should have been posed in such 'adult' poses, but the title of the Vogue article perhaps says it all: 'French Vogue Fashion Spread Features Sexy Sexy Children'. This is an older age group than *Toddlers in Tiaras*, but it is as though Lolita has been reinvented to be younger and younger. What is interesting and concerning about this issue of *Vogue* is that this is not portrayed as a specialist taste; this is representative of how girls should be.

I want to switch tack but I want to talk a little bit about another pincer movement related to the commercialisation of the body, which is the introduction of the body mass index (BMI)[1] and the construction of obesity as a disease entity, which happens to have come from the combined efforts of the pharmaceutical and the diet industry under the rubric of the International Obesity Task Force (IOTF) (see Chapter 4 of Orbach 2009), which sounds very respectable because it is part of the World Health Organization, but is actually, in my opinion, a nefarious group that manages to create a particular kind of conversation around obesity because there is a lot of money to be made by making people feel that they are really not OK in their bodies.

FIGHTBACKS

There is a relationship between the mass eating problems that show, like anorexia and so-called obesity, and the ones that don't show, such as bulimia, compulsive eating, restrained eating and so on. These other kinds of eating problems are less visible but affect more people than obesity. The efforts of organisations like IOTF are percolating through our schools and making an assault on children as young as seven, so that children are being told that they are overweight and on their way to being obese. Their parents are being threatened or shamed about their children's eating and in an extension of this madness, the state of Georgia in the US has put children of size on billboards to humiliate them. This is akin to what is going on in the Southern States around reproductive rights, where people opposed to abortion are doing visual representations of foetuses in a similar attempt to shame women by insisting they have a sonogram of their foetus in 3D so that they really know what they are doing.

These kinds of revolting campaigns are so obviously offensive that people are contesting them and fighting back. There have been women and men who have been sticking pictures on the internet and in schools of their children with the slogan 'For the right to love myself inside and out'. This is a really important campaign and I think we should be looking at the Georgia example because I believe it is a possibility of what is coming to the UK, again, a form of child abuse.

---

1   You cannot go to the doctor now and get contraception without being asked for your BMI. It is a totally irrelevant measure. It was a statistical whimsy that was appropriated for purposes related to commercial exploitation.

Pinkstinks is a London group that has been fighting against the new pink Lego, a Lego that isn't as complicated to put together as the now 'boy's Lego'. I don't know how Lego figured that one out – we women are supposed to be so nimble that we can do needlework, but somehow not nimble enough to do Lego? The Endangered Bodies group (www.endangeredbodies.org) I belong to works in various ways to challenge body hatred foisted on girls and women (and increasingly, boys). We have a campaign called Ditching Dieting (ditching_dietinglondon.endageredbodies.org); we are working with young women in schools and youth clubs to not simply deconstruct and understand the negative influence of visual culture but to reshape it along their own desires (www. shapeyourculture.org.uk), and we work with Campaign for Body Confidence, a parliamentary group composed of other body activists from the worlds of fashion, research, sports, family policy and so on, in order to expand rather than constrain the possibilities for girls and boys and women and men.

In a recent session I had with a mother of a six-year-old girl, the mother said to me, 'You know I really don't think I want my daughter to go to this new birthday party – a "make me a model" party. The parent takes over a beauty salon, has two manicurists, two hairdressers, lighting and catwalk.' In despair the mother wondered how she could handle it so that her daughter did not get the wrong message on the one hand, and on the other hand didn't feel like she could not partake in culture. These are dilemmas and challenges of things I don't think we customarily consider as a form of child abuse, but perhaps we should ask whether they might be.

REFERENCES

Daily Mail (2011) 'Far too much, far too young: Outrage over shocking images of the 10-YEAR-OLD model who has graced the pages of Vogue.' Available at: www. dailymail.co.uk/femail/article-2022305/Thylane-Lena-Rose-Blondeau-Shocking-images-10-YEAR-OLD-Vogue-model.html, accessed 4 July 2013.

Eichenbaum, L. and Orbach, S. (1982) *Understanding Women*. London and New York: Penguin.

Orbach, S. (2009) *Bodies*. London: Profile Books.

Orbach, S. (2011) ' Face to Face.' *Huffington Post*, 6 July.

Orbach, S. and Eichenbaum, L. (1984) *What Do Women Want?* New York: Berkeley Books.

YouTube (2013) 'Still face experiment: Dr Edward Tronick.' Available at www. youtube.com/watch?v=apzXGEbZht0, accessed on 28 April 2013.

CHAPTER 8

GROOMING OUR GIRLS

HYPERSEXUALIZATION OF THE CULTURE AS CHILD SEXUAL ABUSE

DR GAIL DINES

In the spring of 2009 I was sitting in a prison, surrounded by child rapists. All of them had been in long-term group therapy, so they knew each other and felt very comfortable explaining in detail how and why they had raped a child. They were all well schooled in the language of therapy and eager to demonstrate just what good students they were. They peppered their sentences with words like triggered, perpetrator, post-traumatic stress disorder (PTSD), dissociation, and recidivism. All seemed to be more upset by the fact that they were in prison than by the reality of the devastation they had wrought on their victims. Most of them talked about the role porn played in their crimes, explaining how their habitual use of hard-core mainstream porn had become boring, and they had ultimately looked for something different, something a little more edgy, dangerous and transgressive. That something turned out to be the rape of a child.

I tell this story not just to point out the relationship between pornography and violence, but also to introduce you to one of the rapists whom I will call "Dick." Smug, unapologetic, and narcissistic, Dick dominated the conversation with his story of how he set about grooming his ten-year-old stepdaughter, a process, he said, that was not that difficult, since, "the culture did a lot of the grooming for me." I almost jumped out of my seat in shock.

Because I have been doing this work for many years, what stunned me was not the horror of the story (I have heard this over and over from the victims) but the clarity of his thinking. I had been struggling with trying to understand how the hypersexualization and pornification of the culture was shaping the identity of girls and young women, and not one academic or therapist had managed to put it as succinctly as Dick: the culture was acting as a collective perpetrator, and our girls were being collectively groomed for sexual victimization.

THE CULTURE AS PERPETRATOR

Take a stroll through pop culture, and what you'll see are images of a hypersexualized, young, thin, toned, hairless, technologically—and in many cases surgically—enhanced young woman with a come-hither look on her face. We all recognize the look: slightly parted glossy lips, head tilted to the side, inviting eyes, and a body contorted to give the (presumed male) viewer maximum gazing rights to her body. Britney, Rhianna, Beyoncé, Paris, Katy, Lindsay, Kim, Miley, and the thousands of nameless models who stare out from the pages of women's magazines, represent images of contemporary idealized femininity—in a word, hot—that are held up for women, especially young women, to emulate.

In today's image-based culture, there is no escaping the image and no respite from its power when it is relentless in its visibility. If you think I am exaggerating, then flip through a magazine at the supermarket checkout, channel surf, take a drive to look at billboards, or watch TV ads. These images have now normalized the female body as a commodity that exists to be examined, scrutinized, dissected, and emulated. And this female body is getting younger. In 2011, ten-year-old Thylane Blondeau seductively posed on a bed for the French edition of *Vogue*, and Abercrombie & Fitch's 2011 spring line included the "Ashley" bikini top (geared toward children as young as eight), which comes with thick padding for breast enhancement.

People not immersed in pop culture tend to assume that what we see today is just more of the same stuff that previous generations grew up on. After all, every generation has had its hot and sultry stars who led expensive and wild lives compared with the rest of us.

But what is different today is not only the hypersexualization of the image, but also the degree to which such images have overwhelmed and crowded out any alternative images of being female. Today's tidal wave of soft-core porn images has normalized the porn-star look in everyday culture to such a degree that anything less looks dowdy, prim, and downright boring. Today a girl or young woman looking for an alternative to the hypersexualized look will soon come to the grim realization that the only alternative to looking "fuckable" is to be invisible.

Media targeted at girls and women creates a social reality that is so overwhelmingly consistent that it is almost a closed system of messages. In this way, it is the sheer ubiquity of the hypersexualized images that gives them power, since they normalize and publicize a coherent story about femininity and sexuality. Because these messages are everywhere, they take on an aura of such familiarity that we believe them to be our very own personal and individual ways of thinking. They have the power to seep into the core part of our identities to such a degree that we think that we are freely choosing to look and act a certain way because it makes us feel confident, desirable, and happy. But, as scholar Rosalind Gill (2009, p.106) points out, if the look were, "the outcome of everyone's individual, idiosyncratic preferences, surely there would be greater diversity, rather than a growing homogeneity organized round a slim, toned, hairless body."

Understanding the culture as a socializing agent requires exploring how and why some girls and young women conform and others resist. For all of this visual onslaught, not every young woman looks or acts as if she has just tumbled out of the pages of this month's *Cosmopolitan* or *Maxim*. One of the reasons for this is that conforming to a dominant image is not an all-or-nothing act, but rather a series of acts that locate different women and girls at different points on the continuum of conformity to non-conformity. Where any individual sits at any given time on this continuum depends on her past and present experiences, as well as family relationships, media consumption, peer group affiliations, and sexual, racial, and class identity. We are not, after all, blank slates onto which images are projected.

Given the complex ways that we form our sexual and gender identities, it is almost impossible to predict with precision how any individual will act at any one time. This does not mean, though, that we can't make predictions on a macro level. What we can say is that the more one way of being female is elevated above and beyond others, the more a substantial proportion of the population will gravitate toward that which is most socially accepted, condoned, and rewarded. The more the hypersexualized image crowds out other images of women and girls, the fewer options females have of resisting what cultural critic Neil Postman (1990) called "the seduction of the eloquence of the image."

Conforming to the image is seductive. It not only offers women and girls an identity that is in keeping with the majority, but also a whole host of "pleasures," since looking hot does, in fact, garner the kind of male attention that can sometimes feel empowering. Indeed, getting people to consent to any system, even if it's inherently oppressive, is made easier if conformity brings with it psychological, social, and/or material gains. But conformity comes with a price. Girls and young women who "over-conform" to these hypersexualized images get labeled "sluts," and studies show that they "often resort to self-destructive behaviors such as drug and alcohol abuse, eating disorders, self-mutilation, academic withdrawal, or risky sexual conduct."

Wendy Walter-Bailey and Jesse Goodman (2006, p.282) found that the most likely girls to be labeled as sluts are those who, "act too casual and/or flaunt their sexuality" as well as those who, "flirt too heavily, blossom too early, or dress too scantily." But here's the problem in a hypersexualized society: conforming to mainstream norms means girls and young women have to engage in the very behaviors that get them labeled a slut. This is what feminist philosopher Marilyn Frye calls the classic double bind of the oppressed in that they are faced with, "situations in which options are reduced to a very few and all of them expose one to penalty, censure or deprivation" (2007, p.55).

The American Psychological Association's study on the sexualization of girls (2007) found that there was ample evidence to conclude that sexualizing girls, "has negative effects in a variety of domains, including cognitive functioning, physical and mental health, sexuality, and attitudes and beliefs." Some of these effects include more risky sexual behavior, higher rates of eating disorders, depression, and low self-esteem, as well as reduced academic performance. These symptoms are also found in girls and women who have been sexually assaulted, so we appear to be turning out a generation of girls who have been assaulted by the very culture they live in. While some girls and women manage to live their lives without being sexually assaulted by an individual perpetrator, there is no avoiding the culture. The very act of socialization involves internalizing cultural norms and attitudes. If indeed the culture is now one big collective perpetrator, then we can assume that an ever-increasing number of girls and women are going to develop emotional, cognitive, and sexual problems as they are socialized into seeing themselves as mere sex objects, and not much else.

But pop culture is only part of the story of the sexualization of girls. If we look at pornography, which has now become the major form of sex education in the Western world, we see a growing niche market that involves youthful-looking adult women being depicted in ways that sexualize female children and present them as eager and ripe for sex with adult men. The reason for this is that since the advent of the internet, mainstream pornography has become increasingly accessible, violent, and cruel, and this has led to market saturation. One of the only peer-reviewed, empirical studies on the content of mainstream internet porn found that the majority of scenes from 50 of the top-rented porn movies contained both physical and verbal abuse targeted against the female performers. Physical aggression, which included spanking, open-hand slapping, and gagging, occurred in over 88 percent of scenes, while expressions of verbal aggression—calling the woman names such as "bitch" or "slut"—were found in 48 percent of the scenes. The researchers concluded that if both physical and verbal aggression were combined, 90 percent of scenes contained at least one aggressive act (Bridges *et al.* 2010).

Research (see Zillman and Weaver 1989) has found that the problem for the pornographers is that consumers become increasingly desensitized to hard-core porn and are always on the lookout for something new and fresh. Porn director Jules Jordan, who is known for a particularly violent brand of porn, said that even he is, "always trying to figure out ways to do something different," since the fans "are becoming a lot more demanding about wanting to see the more extreme stuff" (2003, p.60). So one of the big challenges pornographers constantly grapple with is how to keep their customers interested.

It is this need to constantly find new niche products that provides insight into why, in 2002, the Free Speech Coalition (the lobbying organization for the porn industry in the USA) worked to change the 1996 Child Pornography Prevention Act, which prohibited any image that, "is, or appears to be, of a minor engaging in sexually explicit conduct." Arguing that the "appears-to-be" language limited the free speech of the pornographers, the Coalition succeeded in removing this "limitation," and the law was narrowed to cover only those images in which an actual person (rather than one who appears to be) under the age of 18 was involved in the making of the porn. Thus, the path was cleared for the porn industry to use either computer-generated images of children or real porn performers who, although aged 18 or over, are "childified" to look much younger.

Since that 2002 decision, there has been an explosion in the number of sites that childify women, as well as those that use computer-generated imagery. Pseudo child pornography (PCP) sites that use adults (those defined by law as 18 years of age or over) to represent children are never called child pornography by the industry. Instead, almost all of those sites that childify the female porn performer are found in the sub-genre called "teen-porn" or "teen-sex" by the industry. There are any number of ways to access these sites, the most obvious one being through Google. Typing "teen porn" into Google yields over 30 million hits, giving the user his choice of thousands of porn sites. A number of the hits are actually for porn portals where "teen porn" is one sub-category of many, and when the user clicks on that category, a list of sites comes up that runs over 90 pages. Moreover, teen porn has its very own portal, which lists hundreds of sub-sub-genres such as "pissing teens," "drunk teens," "teen anal sluts," and "Asian teens."

The competition for customers is fierce in the porn industry, since the user, sitting at his computer and eager to begin his masturbatory session, has a cornucopia of sites, themes, images, and narratives to choose from. The pornographers know this, so they attempt to pull the user in quickly by giving the sites names that are short, to the point, and unambiguous. It is therefore not surprising that many of the sites in this category actually have the word "teen" in the name. When the user clicks on any one of these sites, the first and most striking feature is the body shape of the female porn performers. In place of the large-breasted, curvaceous bodies that populate regular porn websites, one sees small-breasted, slightly built women with adolescent-looking faces that are relatively free of makeup. Many of these performers do look younger than 18, but they do not look like children, so the pornographers use a range of techniques to make them appear more childlike than they actually are. Primary among these is the use of childhood clothes and props such as stuffed animals, lollipops, pigtails, pastel-colored ribbons, ankle socks, braces on the teeth, and, of course, the school uniform. It is not unusual to see a female porn performer wearing a school uniform, sucking a lollipop, and hugging a teddy bear while she masturbates with a dildo.

Another technique for childifying the woman's body is the removal of all pubic hair so that the external genitalia look like that of a pre-pubescent female. What is interesting is that over the years, this technique has lost much of its signifying power, as it is now commonplace in porn for women to remove all their pubic hair. One of the results of this is that today, virtually every female porn performer looks like a child. This is a shift that in itself is cause for concern, as those porn users who are not looking for pseudo-child images nonetheless are exposed to them when they surf the porn sites. This normalization of a shaved pubic area is filtering down increasingly into mainstream pop culture, with regular articles in women's magazines discussing the best way to remove pubic hair, TV shows such as *Sex and the City* publicizing and eroticizing the Brazilian bikini wax, and beauty salons across the country promoting the Brazilian as a way to spice up sex.

The effect this is having on adolescent girls was made evident to me when I spoke at the Sexual Assault Nurse Examiner (SANE) conference in Boston in 2007. These nurses administer rape kits on adolescents who are the victims of sexual assault, and one of their tasks is to check for the markers of puberty, with pubic hair being a key marker. However, I was informed that this is no longer effective, as girls are removing the hair as soon as it grows, something that the nurses have never seen before. In my interviews with college-age females, I hear repeatedly that pubic hair is considered unhygienic and a sexual turnoff by their boyfriends, so they now wax or shave. This is probably one of the clearest examples of how a porn-generated practice slips into the lives of real women, no doubt because a good percentage of the male partners have become accustomed to and aroused by images of women in porn.

For all of the visual clues of childhood surrounding the women on PCP sites, however, it is the written text accompanying the images that does most of the work in convincing the user that he is masturbating to images of sexual activity involving a minor. The words used to describe the women's bodies (including their vaginas)—tiny, small, petite, tight, cute, teeny—not only stress their youthfulness but also work to separate them from women on other sites, since these are adjectives rarely used to describe women in regular porn. Most striking is how many of these PCP sites refer to the females as sweeties, sweethearts, little darlings, cutie pies, honeys—terms of endearment that starkly contrast with the abusive names the women on other sites are called (slut, whore, cumdumpster, and cunt being the most popular). The use of kinder terms on the PCP sites is a method of preserving the notion for the user that these girls are somehow different from the rest of the women who populate the world of porn in that they are not yet used-up whores deserving of verbal abuse. This would explain why so many of these websites have the word "innocent" in their names.

The reason innocence is so central to the marketing of the sites and why the girls are portrayed as not yet sullied, dirtied, soiled, or tainted by sex is that the promise on offer is a witnessing of their loss of innocence. One fan of this genre, writing to a porn discussion forum, calls this a, "knowing innocence," which he defines as, "the illusion of innocence giving way to unbridled sexuality. Essentially, this is the old throwback of the Madonna and the Whore. Therein lies the vast majority of my attraction to this genre." This fan and indeed many others (if their posts are to be believed) make clear that for them, the pleasure is in watching the (sweet, cute, petite) Madonna being coaxed, encouraged, and manipulated by adult men into revealing the whore that lies beneath the (illusory) innocence.

The pornographers reveal their understanding of the nature of this spectatorial pleasure when they offer the guarantee to their consumers that the "girls" they are watching are, "first timers," having their, "first sexual experience," which, of course, leads to their, "first orgasm ever." One site goes so far as to promise that, "Here you will ONLY find the cutest teen girls… Our girls are fresh and inexperienced and very sexy in an innocent kind of way." It is thus no surprise that most of these sites advertise, "fresh girls added each week," since using the same performer twice would cut into the sexual excitement of the viewer. How, after all, does one defile an already-defiled girl?

The story of the "defilement" told on these sites is genre-bound in that it almost always starts with an eager but innocent girl who is gently and playfully coaxed by off-camera adult men into performing sexually for the pleasure of the viewer. This is the narrative informing most of the images on one site, which has hundreds of movies available to members, as well as hundreds of still photographs posted on the site as a teaser for non-members. Each woman has five photographs and a written text detailing her supposed first sexual experience. For "Natasha" the story goes as follows:

> This lil cutie came in pretending that she couldn't wait to be naked in front of the camera. And…we couldn't wait to see her. As she started to take off her clothes and show off she giggled and smiled but we could tell she was nervous and when she found out that naked meant showing off her snug little teen pussy she blushed! But showing off her pussy proved to be too much of a turn on and when we encouraged her to play with it she could not resist. This beautiful teen girl really did have her first time on camera and we got to watch her stroke that velvety teen pussy.

The message that the written text conveys in this story can be found throughout the websites in this category, as it embodies the way in which the pornographers carefully craft a story of who is really innocent and who is really culpable in the scenario. For all the supposed innocence of the "lil cutie," as evidenced by her nervousness, giggling, smiling, and blushing, it really only took a bit of encouragement to get her to masturbate for the camera, which in porn-world language is another way of saying that it didn't take much for her to reveal the slut she really is. It is this very culpability on the part of the girl that simultaneously divests the user of his culpability in masturbating to what would be, in reality, a scenario of adult men manipulating a naive girl into masturbating for the pleasure of other adult men, himself included.

This desire on the part of users to convince themselves that they are masturbating to images of consensual thrilling sex explains the narrative found in another popular PCP sub-genre, namely, incest porn. The sites that sexualize and legitimize incest run the gamut of possible incestuous pairings (mother and son, sibling on sibling, extended family, etc.), but without doubt, the most common portrayal is of a father and daughter. While it is clear that any sexual relationship between a father and his minor daughter is rape, the sites go to great lengths to provide the user with an alternative framing of father–daughter incest. This is especially clear on one site, where the first thing on the home page is the following "explanation":

> The disapproval of incest, especially between father and daughter, is a classic example of "projection." The alleged reason for diasproval [sic] is that incest is the same as sexual abuse, aggression and violence. These are all rational arguments, but they are used to justify an irrational opinion. In fact, most cases of incest have little to do with violence.

Indeed, if these sites are to be believed, then incest is what happens when a seductive and manipulative "daughter" finally gets her reluctant "father" to succumb to her sexual advances. On one site, the reader is invited to watch, "sexy naughty girls seducing their own fathers," and on another, the female performers are defined as, "sweet, irresistible angels teasing and tempting their own daddies." Another site asks the user to, "check out forbidden love stories," where sexually curious daughters are eying their fathers' bodies with lust. A typical story line reads:

> I have fancied my father for years. I thought it was a perversion and was afraid to reveal my emotions…. Once I saw him in a wet dream. This was a sign. Still half asleep I went into his room and jumped onto his bed…

Of course, it doesn't take much to get the father to acquiesce, and surrounding the text are images of the "daughter" being penetrated orally, anally, and vaginally by the "father."

In those stories where the father is seen as the active seducer, the girls are generally only too happy to oblige. Once the sexual "relationship" begins, it is clear that the sex was better than either one could ever have imagined. Even in those occasional stories where the daughter is somewhat afraid, the end result is orgasmic sex. In one story a "daughter" explains that:

my mom died 3 years ago. Since then dad never brought home a woman. Soon I started noticing very strange looks he gave me. I was even a little afraid. One evening dad came to my room. I was sitting on my bed. He approached me and…

A sequence of eight images surrounding the text tell the story of a clothed, anxious girl succumbing to the sexual advances of the father and ending up naked and orgasmic on a bed. What stands out in this story, and indeed in most of the scenarios on these sites, is the absence of a mother to protect the daughter from the father's abuse. Some of the scenarios like the above describe her as dead, but most make no reference to a mother at all, thus creating a family scene where the girl is isolated and at the mercy of the perpetrating father. This lack of a mother is actually not unusual in cases of father–daughter incest. Indeed, as Judith Herman found in her study (2000), over half the sexually abused girls she interviewed had mothers who were absent from the daily routine of the family due to ill health or death. In these families, Herman describes fathers who are controlling and patriarchal, "as the family providers, they felt they had the right to be nurtured and served at home, if not by their wives, then by their daughters." For some of these fathers, being "nurtured" extended to being sexually serviced by their daughters, who were turned into surrogate wives even though they were physically and mentally children. Of course, the real-life consequences of such abuse look nothing like the fairy tale world of incest porn, since these girls all exhibited numerous symptoms consistent with PTSD.

The reduction of the daughter to an object to be used by the father is most stark on one particular site (the banner reads: "Want to Fuck My Daughter?"), which tells the story of a drunken father pimping out his daughter to any man who will pay. The images and the sex in the films are standard hard-core porn, but the stories that contextualize the images tell a story of economic degradation and poverty, with the way out being the prostituting of a daughter. The text introducing the site reads:

Meet my daughter Janessa, she's 19 years old and like her mom, she is so freakin' hot. And its no fucking secret to the world that she loves to fuck. What a fucking slut! i think she got that from her mom. God damn her womb is so polluted. aaanyways.

My daughter fucks some stupid guys anywhere she goes. I was like WTF!? for free? Shit! I didn't raise her to get fucked for free! Well, im a bum old, and im always fucking wasted so fuck that, now i let her fuck any guy she wants as long as the guy pays me some cash bucks… Aww fuck that, why dont you hit join now!!! Watch this slut take cocks for cash in my pockets.

The "daughter"—or slut, as the father constantly refers to her—is depicted as an active and willing player in the scenarios, often leaving her father by the roadside as she speeds off with the latest "john". The text makes constant reference to the father's drinking and poverty as a way to minimize his culpability in turning his daughter into a prostitute, and also finds a way to put the blame on the absent mother by mentioning her "polluted" womb.

All the sites discussed so far depict scenarios in which the men do not use overt force to get the girl to comply with their sexual demands, but rather seduce, manipulate, and cajole the girl into submission. This picture actually mirrors what goes on in the real world of child molestation, as most of the victims are subject to a grooming process wherein the perpetrator first seduces the child with gifts, affection, calculated acts of kindness, and offers of friendship and/or mentoring. Having forged a bond, the perpetrator then manipulates and exploits the emotional connection to erode the child's resistance to sexual activity and to ensure the child's silence. For perpetrators, this is a safer way than overt force, since it does not leave visible scars, and because it is an act of breaking the child's will, the victim is more likely to keep the abuse hidden for fear of appearing disloyal to the perpetrator. Moreover, the bond acts as a kind of glue for the child, keeping her/him connected even when the adult is perpetrating awful acts of sexual violence. The pornographers are well aware of this grooming process, since they do an excellent job of depicting it in their movies by showing a whole range of techniques—from gift giving to strategic acts of kindness, where the perpetrator poses as a kind (sexual) mentor. Always brazen, the pornographers constantly use the word "breaking" to refer to what they are doing to the girls.

The obvious question here is: what effect could these sites have on the viewers? Once they click on these sites, users are bombarded—through images and words—with an internally consistent ideology that legitimizes, condones, and celebrates a sexual desire for children. The norms and values that circulate in society that define adult–child sex as deviant and abusive are wholly absent in PCP, and in their place is a cornucopia of sites that deliver the message (to the viewer's brain, via the penis), that sex with children is hot fun for all.

There is a wealth of research within media studies that shows that people construct their notions of reality from the media they consume, and the more consistent and coherent the message, the more people believe it to be true. Thus, the images of girls in PCP do not exist within a social vacuum, but rather are produced and consumed within a society where the dominant pop culture images are of childified women and hypersexualized, youthful female bodies. Encoded within all of these images is an ideology that encourages the sexual objectification of the female body, an ideology that is internalized by both males and females, and has become so widespread that it normalizes the sexual use and abuse of females. This does not mean that all men who masturbate to PCP will rape a child, or even be sexually attracted to a child. What it does mean, however, is that on a cultural level, when we sexualize the female child, we chip away at the norms that define children as off limits to male sexual use. The more we undermine such cultural norms, the more we drag girls into the category of "woman," and in a porn-saturated world, to be a woman is to be a sexual object deserving of male contempt, use, and abuse.

REFERENCES

APA (American Psychological Association) (2007) *Sexualization of Girls*. Washington, DC: APA. Available at www.apa.org/pi/women/programs/girls/report.aspx, accessed on 20 May 2013.

Bridges, A., Wosnitzer, R., Scharrer, E., Sun, C. and Liberman, R. (2010) 'Aggression and sexual behavior in best-selling pornography videos: A content analysis update.' *Violence Against Women, 16*, 10, 1065–1085.

Frye, M. (2007) 'Oppression.' In P. Rothenberg (ed.) *Race, Class, and Gender in the United States*. New York: Worth.

Gill, R. (2009) 'Supersexualize Me! Advertising and the Midriff.' In F. Attwood, *Mainstreaming Sex*. London: I.B. Tauris.

Herman, J. (2000) *Father–Daughter Incest*. Cambridge, MA: Harvard University Press.

Jordan, J. (2003) *Adult Video News*, January.

Postman, N. (1990) *Consuming Images*. PBS Video.

Walter-Bailey, W. and Goodman, J. (2006) 'Exploring the Culture of Sluthood among Adolescents.' In *Contemporary Youth Culture: An International Encyclopedia*. Westport, CT: Greenwood.

Zillmann, D. and Weaver, J.B. (1989) 'Pornography and Men's Sexual Callousness Toward Women.' In D. Zillmann and J. Bryant (eds) *Pornography: Research Advances and Policy Considerations* (pp.95–125). Hillsdale, NJ: Lawrence Erlbaum Associates, Inc.

CHAPTER 9

THE INTERNET

A GLOBAL MARKET FOR CHILD SEXUAL ABUSE

SHARON GIRLING OBE

In this chapter, I describe some headline statistics relating to the scale of internet use and abuse, as well as some of my experiences at the forefront of combating child abuse and pornography on the internet as a Detective Constable for the National Crime Squad involved in the case of Operation Cathedral – a police operation that broke up an international child pornography ring called The Wonderland Club operating over the internet.

SOME FACTS AND FIGURES

The internet is a global phenomenon that has clearly changed, for the better, the lives of the majority its users. In the year 2000 the world population was 6,115,000,000 of which 360,985,492 had internet access; this is fewer than 6 per cent. By 2011 the world population was 6,973,738,433 of which 2,405,518,376 had internet access; this is greater than 34 per cent (International Telecommunication Union 2011).

The World Wide Web has given people of all ages, vulnerabilities and ethnicity the ability to:

• access news and sports reports as they happen

• learn more about their specific interest

- shop without the hassle of travelling, parking and queuing
- conduct their financial activity online
- book a holiday
- interact socially with family and friends all over the world instantly
- work from their homes, and many other things.

People who were previously isolated or lonely now report that they use the internet as an outlet, and in most instances they have found someone who listens and engages with them – someone to share their stories with. Even if this is not a verbal or physical communication it is a communication none the less.

However, the downside to this technology is that people who prey on the young and vulnerable now have the capacity to seek them out and groom them for their own benefit. One such person was David Hines, now a registered sex offender. Hines was convicted for his role in The Wonderland Club, a case investigated under the code name of Operation Cathedral. Hines lived alone and downloaded thousands of images of child abuse. He did not think that having a sexual relationship with a child was wrong. When interviewed for a BBC documentary, Hines stated:

> It's great the net. New pictures to trade…it's wonderful – it draws you in, it sucks you in. It's a whole world in itself. I had people I could talk to. I had people that I could trade images with as well. But I had friends. I'd never had so many friends. I had friends all over the world. There were some children…we just didn't see it as abuse. We saw it as there were some children involved in relationships. (BBC Panorama 2001)

DEFINING SEXUAL EXPLOITATION

The term 'sexual exploitation' is an all-encompassing statement. Depending on the organisation, agency or individual person, its definition will change. This is very confusing and potentially dangerous for children, young people and vulnerable adults.

The National Society for the Prevention of Cruelty to Children (NSPCC) defines sexual exploitation as: '...when someone grooms and controls a child for a sexual purpose' (www.nspcc.org.uk).

Whereas Barnardo's states that: 'It is illegal activity by people who have power over young people and use it to sexually abuse them' (www.barnardos.org.uk).

And the United Nations defines it as: '...any actual or attempted abuse of a position of vulnerability, differential power, or trust, for sexual purposes, including, but not limited to, profiting monetarily, socially or politically from the sexual exploitation of another' (United Nations no date).

It is important to note that many agencies direct the term solely towards children and not necessarily young or vulnerable adults. To include these groups, perhaps a suitable definition may be: 'A person taking sexual advantage of another for their own benefit or gain.'

The NSPCC reports that one in six children has been sexually abused by the time they are 16. As a child born in the 1960s I was brought up hearing about the danger of strangers from family and teachers. We were all wary of the man in the raincoat in the park and reminded that we should never take sweets from a stranger. But the NSPCC informs us that the essence of the stranger is applicable to only 20 per cent. They highlight that eight out of ten children (a staggering 80%) know their abuser, that is, it wasn't a stranger at all.

This statistic should increase substantially the number of children rescued from abuse and escalate the number of abusers brought to account. However, it appears that the vast majority of children who are abused do not disclose the matter to any third party, and this is a failing on society as a whole and not just the police or social services.

A study published in 2012 by the Office of the Children's Commissioner identified 2409 victims of sexual abuse in a period of 14 months leading to October 2011. It further reported a further 16,500 children who were at, 'high risk of sexual exploitation' in 2010–11. The question should be asked why these vulnerable children are not feeling safe enough to confide in an adult.

It is important to ensure that reports and definitions relating to sexual exploitation include the terms 'young people and vulnerable adults' as well as 'children'. In some instances the abuser's sexual interest is increased by the vulnerability of the victim and not necessarily their age. I can recall a case where the offender engaged in a physical relationship with a severely vulnerable adult where his sexual needs were met and yet he downloaded indecent images of young boys and girls.

CHILD SEX OFFENDING STATISTICS

There was an enormous increase in reported child sex offending in England and Wales between 2005 and 2010. Compare the increase in the world population's access to the internet (34%), to the increase in these reported crimes and the numbers are horrifying: a 60 per cent increase in child sex offending between 2005 and 2010.

YEAR	NUMBER OF PEOPLE CAUTIONED OR CONVICTED FOR OFFENCES RELATING TO INDECENT IMAGES OF CHILDREN
2005	1,363
2006	1,675
2007	1,747
2008	1,888
2009	1,916
2010	2,135
Total	10,724

Source: Cafe (2011)

In 2000 the number of people cautioned or convicted for offences relating to indecent images of children was 303. In the year 2009 the number had risen to 1,916, an increase of more than 600 per cent (Cafe 2011).

The National Child Abuse hotline states that every year 3.3 million reports of child abuse are made in the US involving nearly six million children. They advise that 9.2 per cent of those reports relate to sexual abuse (303,600,000) whilst 17.6 per cent relate to physical abuse (580,800,000) (Childhelp no date).

WHO ARE THE ABUSERS?

Having determined that the abusers are not strangers, it will still come as a shock as to who the abusers are. You only have to recall the case in Plymouth at Little Ted's Nursery. The abusers Vanessa George (nursery school worker), Angela Allen (traffic warden) and Colin Blanchard (IT consultant) met on Facebook and started to message each other via text and email. The messages became sexually explicit and George took indecent pictures of her own 14-year-old daughter as well as some of the children aged two to five years from the nursery school where she worked, and sent them to Blanchard and Allen. The three of them also befriended two other women online, Tracy Lyons and Tracy Dawber (community care worker).

This case was uncovered by a colleague of Blanchard's who saw the sexually explicit images of toddlers and babies on Blanchard's computer whilst looking for some business files. The four women and one man were arrested by the police and convicted of various offences including sexual assault of a minor, making indecent photographs of children and distributing indecent photographs of children.

In a case in the UK, known as Operation Ore, the occupations of the offenders who were found in possession of indecent images was incredible. There were over 50 people who worked within the police service as either sworn officers or civilian staff. There was a similar number from the teaching profession, social care environment and those working with children via the voluntary sector.

When you consider the occupations of these offenders and the position of trust they hold, it is no wonder that children provide the following reasons for not reporting the abuse they are subjected to:

• 'was frightened'

• 'didn't think would be believed'

• 'had been threatened by abuser'

• 'didn't want parents to find out'

• 'didn't want friends to find out'

• 'didn't want the authorities to find out'

- 'didn't think it was serious or wrong'

- 'it was nobody else's business'.

THE HISTORY

So where did it start?

In 1996–97 one police force in the UK recovered 12 images of child abuse from one case. As a member of the public I find myself asking the question, 'Should we have considered this a problem?' As a retired police officer I answer my question with, 'Probably not.' But little did I, or the rest of the policing community, know what lurked around the corner. From early 1998 my career became focused on policing online child abuse and to date this is still the case.

In early 1996 a US citizen created a private group known as the Orchid Club in which its members told each other stories about their sexual contact with children and sent each other, via the internet, indecent images of children. During this time one of the members, Ronald Riva, had been sexually abusing a friend of his young daughter and he verbally and pictorially shared the abuse with the other members of the Orchid Club. Some of the members requested that the child perform 'live' over the internet. The abuser sought advice from one member of the group on how to teach the young girl to insert a vibrator and suggestions were received.

In April 1996 the live online abuse of the girl took place via a computer webcam programme known as CU-SeeMe and the abuse was broadcast to all the other invited members. The molestation and subsequent images included the girl having a vibrator inserted into her vagina. The other members replied with requests for further sexual acts. The abuser assaulted other young girl friends of his daughter and one of them reported the incident.

The police arrested Riva and his associate Melton Myers and searched their home addresses including their computers. Both men received custodial sentences. An examination of the computer seized from Riva led to the identity of the other members of the Orchid Club, three of whom were UK citizens.

The first was arrested and no evidence was located on his computer to support the allegations. The second was arrested and although he admitted that he had paedophilic material on his computer, none was found. He was released without charge. This man was later arrested and convicted for the rape of his two-year-old daughter following images of the abuse being located on the computers of other offenders. The third man, Ian Baldock, a computer consultant, was arrested at his home in Sussex in October 1997. His computers were examined and police located in excess of 42,000 indecent images of children. In the six days leading to his arrest he had disseminated 1642 images to 17 internet users. He had logged the activity on his computer of members of the Orchid Club as well as The Wonderland Club, of which he was also a member.

This club had approximately 180 members worldwide from countries including the US, Australia, the Netherlands, Portugal, Italy, France, Austria, Germany, Denmark, Sweden, Belgium, Canada and Norway. In some of the countries it was not an offence to possess these images because they did not realise these images existed.

The Wonderland Club was a group of men, all who had a sexual interest in children. It had the following membership rules:

- Each member must possess at least 10,000 unique child abuse images.

- Each member must agree to distribute those images to other members.

- Each member must be introduced and approved by the members.

- A vote was cast between the club management, and if there were any objections, your access was denied.

The Wonderland Club had a good level of security, which was created to stop infiltration from non-members and law enforcement. This included:

- The existence of a secret server.

- The location of the server (IP address).

- A password to log into the server.

- The member must be on the approved list.

- The member must connect from a pre-arranged internet location and a set time.

One of the members from the UK, Gary Salt, was arrested independently in April 1998 for sexual offences against his three stepchildren and a young family friend. The evidence gathered from his computer assisted the investigation.

On 1 September 1998 law enforcement agencies across the globe pulled their resources together and 108 suspects were either arrested or visited at their home addresses simultaneously. (This was dependent on local legislation.) From those arrests, more than 750,000 child abuse images were recovered.

In the UK 12 people were arrested, of which ten were charged. One of the men from the UK committed suicide prior to attending court; the remaining nine were convicted, including David Hines. Their occupations included taxi driver, computer consultants and Royal Aircraftsman. None of them were men in raincoats hanging out at the park or sweetshop. The sentences varied across the globe. In the US they received sentences of up to 30 years' imprisonment and in the UK the longest term of imprisonment was 30 months. The offender Gary Salt was sentenced to 12 years' imprisonment for the rape and sexual assaults on his young victims. At the conclusion of the case, the Government increased the sentencing for those found in possession of indecent images of children and for making or distributing them.

All of the UK offenders have subsequently been released from prison, and a number of them have gone on to re-offend. However, the sentences they received the second, or in some instances the third, time they offended had not been increased. In one instance the offender received a longer prison sentence for travelling overseas than for distributing images of child abuse.

COSTING OF EXAMINATION/ INVESTIGATION

So how much does it cost to conduct an investigation? The UK staffing alone for Operation Cathedral consisted of a detective superintendent, a detective inspector, three detective sergeants, 14 detective constables, two computer consultants, and an administrator. The total cost was in excess of £250,000. The investigation started in April 1998 and was concluded at court in January 2001, taking almost three years. The offenders remained on bail awaiting their trial. The police had very little opportunity to monitor their online activity.

In 1998–2001 in the homes that were searched for offences relating to internet misuse, police found only one or two internet active devices, which were mainly computer towers. In today's society these homes have many more. Not only are there towers, but there are also laptops, tablets, smartphones, game-consoles, televisions and other devices. This gives children, young people and vulnerable adults, as well as offenders, access to the internet whilst they are moving around. It affords those who prey on the vulnerable the opportunity to locate those people and place themselves in a position to engage with them when they are least expecting it. I recall an incident where a voluntary boys' club took a group of its young male members to a national landmark and reported their anticipated activity online along with the names of its participants. A male offender placed himself at that location and identified himself as a relative of another member to one of the young boys. He called him by name and the child accepted the unknown adult male as a person he could trust, and walked away with him.

So, what can be done to minimise the risk of harm to children and young people?

ADVICE FOR PARENTS AND CARERS OF CHILDREN

Whether you are a parent, carer or a young person, the online advice is the same:

- Know what information about yourself and your family you are giving out and to whom you are giving it.

- Parents and carers should get involved in children's online activity at home or elsewhere. It is important to understand what they are doing, the sites they are visiting, the social networking they are members of and the people they are engaging with.

- Encourage internet use that builds on offline activities. Ask the child or young person's school what e-safety tools they use and whether they can be replicated at home. Parents' evenings are a good opportunity to engage with the teachers regarding e-safety.

- Teach children and young people to be SMART:

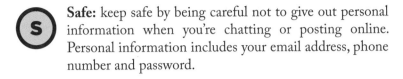

Safe: keep safe by being careful not to give out personal information when you're chatting or posting online. Personal information includes your email address, phone number and password.

Meeting: meeting someone you have only been in touch with online can be dangerous, so it's not a good idea. Only do so with your parents' or carer's permission and even then only when they can be present. Remember online friends are still strangers even if you have been talking to them for a long time.

Accepting: accepting emails, IM messages, or opening files, pictures or texts from people you don't know or trust can lead to problems – they may contain viruses or nasty messages.

Reliable: someone online might lie about who they are. If you are chatting online it's best to only chat to your real world friends and family. Information on the internet may not be true. Always check information with other websites, books or someone who knows.

Tell: tell your parent, carer, trusted adult or Childline (0800 1111) if someone or something makes you feel uncomfortable or worried, or if you or someone you know is being bullied online (www.kidsmart.org.uk).

- Understand that by having the GPS activated on your mobile device it is traceable and there are apps and programmes that allow others to identify where you are. If you upload photographs online the location that the picture was taken is available to others who view that image. So, if your child attends the local sports centre and you take a picture of them and upload it to your Google images, then a third party may identify the location that photograph was taken and arrive at that location the following week.

SOCIAL NETWORKING

Older children could be asked some basic yet thought provoking questions, such as:

- How many social networking sites do you have a profile on?

- How many digits are in your password?

- How often do you check your privacy settings?

- Would be happy to show me your profile now?

- Would you be happy to show your profile to your future employer, college or university?

SOME FACTS AND FIGURES ABOUT SOCIAL NETWORKING

- There are more than 845 million active Facebook users (users returned in last 30 days), of which 55 per cent log on to their profile in any given day.

- Facebook is available in more than 70 languages.

- The average user has 130 friends.

- People (all users) generally spend in excess of 750 billion minutes per month on Facebook.

- More than 7 million apps and websites are integrated with Facebook, and on average people (all users) install apps more than 20 million times every day.

- The platform has had 10 billion photos uploaded, of which 15 billion images are viewed daily.

- The average user is connected to 80 community pages, groups and events.

- More than 350 million active users currently access Facebook through their mobile devices and more than 475 mobile operators globally work to deploy and promote Facebook mobile products.

- If Facebook were a country, it would be the third largest in the world behind China and India (http://newsroom.fb.com).

One in three hiring managers stated that checking social media led to the employee not getting the job, for the following reasons:

- sharing provocative or inappropriate photos (49%)

- sharing information about drinking or drug use (45%)

- poor communication skills (35%)

- bad-mouthing a previous employer (33%)

- discriminatory remarks relating to race, gender or religion (28%)

- lying about qualifications (22%).

Of those potential employers who checked a positive profile:

- Fifty-eight per cent said it gave them a good feel for the candidate's personality

- Fifty-five per cent liked profiles that conveyed a professional image

- Fifty-four per cent said that information they found supported the candidate's professional qualifications

- Fifty-one per cent liked social media profiles that displayed a well-rounded candidate, showing a wide range of interests

- Forty-nine per cent cited great communication skills

- Forty-four per cent said it displayed the candidate's creativity

- Thirty-four per cent said that other people's online recommendations made a difference (http://thenextweb.com/socialmedia/2012/04/18).

Children and young people should be reminded that their profile is how others will see them and that they are at the start of their life and shouldn't be making a basic, life-affecting, social networking mistake. The internet is not like a night out with friends where, 'what happens on the night out with friends stays with friends'. Activity conducted and uploaded onto the internet is there for life!

ADVICE FOR CHILD WELFARE PROFESSIONALS

As a professional there are some basic points to consider, should you suspect indecent images of children are on a person's computer.

Do:

- Inform the police as soon as it is safe to do so.

- Unplug or switch off the device if it is safe to do so.

- Make a note of the time and date, what you saw, the device you saw it on and where the device was at the time.

- Check to see if there is any other information available to support what you have just seen on your internal agency system (have the children or family members mentioned anything previously?).

Do not:

- Look at the images.

- Copy the images.

- Delete the images.

- Do anything on that device.

If you are working with a police officer, be aware that they may not fully understand what to do so be confident to tell them that you have some knowledge.

If you are attending the house with the police to execute a search warrant, remind the police officer to seize all electronic devices including those capable of storing data during the search warrant including:

- cameras

- mobile phones

- computer games consoles

- DVDs

- USB memory sticks.

So what is an indecent image of a child? The Sentencing Council has categorised indecent images of children into five levels of seriousness, with level five being the most serious:

- Level one: images of erotic posing, with no sexual activity.

- Level two: non-penetrative sexual activities between children, or solo masturbation by a child.

- Level three: non-penetrative sexual activity between adults and children.

- Level four: penetrative sexual activity involving a child or children, or both children and adults.

- Level five: sadism or involving the penetration of, or by, an animal.

(The Crown Prosecution Service 2012)

Offenders who are convicted of possessing, making or distributing indecent images are sentenced according the volume of material and the activity in the image (that is, level one to level five).[1]

An additional factor considered at the point of sentencing is the age of the child; if the child in the image is under 13 years and so those examining the images also need to age the child in the pictures.

This is a very time-consuming process and it can take several hours to view the thousands of images recovered from a suspect's computer.

Finally, as a practitioner, remember that there are many others who are doing the same job as you. Every police force has a team dedicated to policing child abuse online and a forensic examination team. Both of these departments are available to assist should you require it. Furthermore, the Child Exploitation and Online Protection Centre also has staff who can advise you.

REFERENCES

BBC Panorama (2001) 'Wickedness of Wonderland.' Available at: http://news. bbc.co.uk/1/hi/uk/1167879.stm, accessed on 4 July 2013.

---

1   R v Oliver, Hartrey Baldwin (2003) [2002] EWCA Crim 2766; R v Oliver, R v Hartrey and R v Baldwin [2003] 1 Cr App R 28.

Cafe, R. (2011) 'Convictions for sex offences on children up 60% in six years.' BBC News. Available at www.bbc.co.uk/news/uk-14596811, accessed on 28 April 2013.

Childhelp (no date) 'National Child Abuse Statistics.' *Childhelp.* Available at www.childhelp.org/pages/statistics, accessed on 28 April 2013.

Crown Prosecution Service (2012) 'Indecent Images of Children.' Available at: http://www.cps.gov.uk/legal/s_to_u/sentencing_manual/indecent_images_of_children/, accessed on 4 July 2013.

International Telecommunication Union (2011) 'The World in 2011 – ICT Facts and Figures.' Available at: http://www.itu.int/en/ITU-D/Statistics/Documents/facts/ICTFactsFigures2011.pdf, accessed on 4 July 2013.

Office of the Children's Commissioner (2012) 'Inquiry into Child Sexual Exploitation in Gangs and Groups – Interim Report.' Available at: http://www.childrenscommissioner.gov.uk/, accessed 4 July 2013.

United Nations (no date) 'Overview.' *Protection from Sexual Exploitation and Abuse.* Available at www.un.org/en/pseataskforce/overview.shtml, accessed on 28 April 2013.

CHAPTER 10

SEX, SEXUALITY AND CHILD SEXUAL ABUSE

PROFESSOR LIZ KELLY CBE

In these days of easy access to current information on the internet it is all too easy to ignore the past. The sexualised representation of women and girls was a focus of feminist critique from the 1970s, with many creative campaigns and actions addressing it. Media representations are the subject of a paragraph in the United Nations (UN) Convention on the Elimination of All Forms of Discrimination Against Women (CEDAW), but sustained work on this issue fell into abeyance from the 1990s, in part due to deep divisions about pornography.

Simultaneously, the issue of children abused through pornography emerged, an arena where consensus was more possible but disconnected from the gender and equalities agenda that underpins CEDAW. A similar disconnection can be traced with respect to sexualisation, where the origin of the concept was a re-awakening of feminist resistance to the (re)sexualisation of popular culture, yet has become increasingly limited in public policy to concerns about the 'early' or 'over' sexualisation of children and young people. In the process we have lost important connections – that this is not just about body image and self-esteem of girls, but how these representations function to normalise attitudes and behaviours that underpin both child sexual abuse and sexual exploitation.

In 2000 we wrote a piece questioning the separation of sexual exploitation of children from the continuum of sexual abuse in childhood. It seems appropriate to revisit that theme over a decade later, especially since there appears to be a painfully short memory of where we have been. Rather than the image of child welfare/ protection being a pendulum swinging between over and under intervention, I prefer the image of a clock face where each number is a dimension of child maltreatment. Over the last four decades only parts of the clock face have been illuminated at any particular time, leaving the others – which continue in children's and young people's lives – in the shadows, only to be 're-discovered' and shed new light on at some later point.

Concerns about the abuse of children in prostitution was a critical issue in the late 19th century and continued in muted form for much of the 20th century. By the end of the 1980s the issue of sexual abuse in the family had been well and truly unearthed again, and in the decade that followed researchers and practitioners began to explore the wider parameters, including what was then called 'organised abuse' – abuse by multiple perpetrators and within institutions – with sexual exploitation then referring to abuse through pornography and prostitution (see Itzin 2000). The arena of the greatest contention in this period was undoubtedly ritual abuse, which traversed all of these categories. The stories that children and adults told were viewed as literally 'incredible' by some agencies and much of the media, with the latter endlessly repeating a myth that the high-profile cases during the 1990s were a 'moral panic'. Yet a number of adults were convicted of sex offences against children in Nottingham and Rochdale: there is no crime of 'ritual abuse' to be convicted of, but both these facts have escaped public consciousness. Since that time there have been further convictions, and in court the ritual and even Satanic elements have been revealed, but with minimal media coverage. Children and adults telling the truth about sexual violation has rarely been considered newsworthy. The disbelief contrasts sharply with the ease with which, in the last decade, ritualised abuse has been accepted when the victims and perpetrators have been from minority groups. We would all benefit from reflecting on these contrasting stories, and what they tell us about the processes of belief, credibility and agency responses.

The understanding of sexual exploitation as child abuse through pornography and prostitution (and more recently trafficking) became a huge global issue, resulting in policy documents from the European Union (EU) and UN, prompted by three World Congresses – the first in 1996 in Sweden, followed by 2001 in Japan and 2008 in Brazil. Many states, including the UK, created plans of action to address sexual exploitation by 2000, drawing on exciting and innovative practice from children's charities, especially Barnardo's and The Children's Society. This history has been virtually invisible in the resurgence of interest in sexual exploitation, which is now framed, through the work of Office of the Children's Commissioner, in terms of exploitation by 'gangs and groups'.

What we need to be alert to here is that clock face – we have moved through thinking in terms of 'sex abuse rings', 'sex abuse networks', 'organised abuse', 'institutional abuse', 'sexual exploitation', 'commercial sexual exploitation': all have different inclusions and exclusions and emphases. Words matter – they direct our attention towards some things and away from others, influencing what we are open to seeing and believing, creating climates of belief and disbelief. This, in turn, has direct consequences for which children and adult survivors feel able to speak and seek help. The Jimmy Savile case has been remarkable and unusual in this respect, since the revelations were unbelievable, and the tired tropes of 'witch hunts' and 'moral panics' were flown by some journalists. Yet a climate of belief sustained and in its wake many hundreds of adults and children chose to tell others what had happened to them. In the process, cases in which rumours about powerful men and organised networks re-surfaced and are being re-investigated.

In the last few months one of the most prominent words across print and spoken media has been 'paedophile rings', a deeply problematic concept that casts large shadows on the clock face. First, the literal meaning of paedophile is 'lover of children' – not an appropriate definition when we are discussing sexual abuse of children. Second, its clinical meaning is someone whose sexual interest is confined to children: yet we know that many offenders – like Savile – also abuse adults. To continually call him a paedophile makes his adult victims at worst invisible, at best less important than the children. Last, the concept serves to otherise and monsterise abusers – they are the strange strangers, not those familiar to children in their everyday lives; yet we all know that the majority of children are sexually abused by those they know – family members, authority figures and peers. We also know that the vast majority of sexual offences against children (and adults) are committed by males. Given that the concept of paedophile sits in tension with most of what we know about sexual abuse, why do so many of us continue to use it?

Some have argued that the Savile case and the revelations that continue to spin out from it represent a 'moment', a possibility of shifting public perceptions about child sexual abuse.

We need to pay close attention to what happens next – each time a bridgehead of belief has been established in the past it begins to be dismantled, and as soon as this happens silence becomes a preferred option for many. Re-building the bridge seems to require beginning in a different place – remember the clock face – with the consequence that something is lost in the process.

My hope is that in this moment we can dare to join up the dots between abuse of children and of women, to keep more of the clock face in view. This has begun, to some extent, through successive governments having strategies on violence against women and girls; but this has yet to translate into recognition of the relevance of a gender perspective in the child welfare and child protection fields. We need a gender perspective that recognises not just that women and girls are disproportionately the victims of sexual exploitation and the targets of sexualised culture, but that men and boys are disproportionately those who exploit and abuse.

REFERENCE

Itzin, C. (ed.) (2000) *Home Truths about Child Sexual Abuse: Influencing Policy and Practice*. London: Routledge.

CHAPTER 11

CHILDREN, CHILDHOOD AND SEXUALISED POPULAR CULTURE

DR MADDY COY

The sexualisation of popular culture as a social issue has exploded into public awareness and onto policy and academic agendas. The contours of the debate have become complex and contested, with definitions of sexualisation, what constitutes 'evidence' of its impact and thus social implications closely scrutinised (see Gill 2011 and Coy and Garner 2012 for overviews). Yet at the same time, the terms of discussion within the media and public discourse, policy frameworks and much academia, have ossified into alarm about the toxicity of 'early' and 'premature' sexualisation for children and young people. From this vantage point, sexualised popular culture is itself not problematic, only the age at which children and young people engage with it. Generation has trumped gender as the pivot around which commentary and campaigning revolve; feminist analyses have become marginalised. Space for a critical perspective on gender that includes interrogation of what messages about being a young woman/man are transmitted through sexualised popular culture has been largely lost.

In this chapter, I reinstate the case for an analysis of sexualised popular culture that recognises the importance of both generation and gender, shifting the tenor of debate beyond populist sound and fury about the contamination of children's innocence. I begin by outlining discussions about how sexualisation is defined and understood, reflect briefly on current policy frameworks and academic perspectives, before exploring the contradictions and confusions of approaches focused simply around 'age-inappropriate' sexualisation. In the final section I suggest how a gendered analysis can be integrated into conversation with young people.

SEXUALISATION: DEFINITIONS AND DISCOURSES

The term 'sexualisation' is invoked to describe the mainstreaming of sexual imagery in contemporary popular culture (Gill 2007). There is little consensus over what constitutes sexualisation and thus to what the term refers, although there is a common recognition that deeply heteronormative sexual imagery and discourse has increased in volume and visibility. Across all elements of 'this image-based culture' – for example, advertising, music videos, lads' mags – 'the staple...is the youthful, sexualised female body' (Dines 2011, p.3). Several feminist commentators have suggested that the term 'pornification' more accurately captures a cultural style in which 'pornographic permutations' (McRobbie 2008), the 'codes and conventions of pornography' are evident (Dines 2011, p.3; Whelehan 2000). These conventions, in brief, include: that women and girls enjoy being sexually available for men and boys; that the most socially prized form of masculinity is defined by sexual conquest; and that this masculinity is shored up by the 'collective consumption of naked women' (Funnell 2011, p.38). Aesthetic codes originating in pornography have also permeated into popular culture and thus become normalised expectations for women and girls' bodies, such as shaved pubic areas and breast enlargement surgery (Coy and Garner 2010; Dines 2011).

Underpinning these conventions are interlinked social narratives about gender. First, is that the achievement of formal equality means that feminism is often perceived as irrelevant and outdated (see Gill 2007; McRobbie 2009). Yet multiple inequalities persist: women are severely under-represented in political decision-making (Fawcett Society 2013); the gender pay gap in the UK is 19.7 per cent between men's and women's average earnings (Office for National Statistics 2012); and violence against women, internationally recognised as a cause and consequence of gender inequality, remains endemic across all communities (End Violence Against Women 2011a; Walby 2011). Discussions about contemporary gender relations, and indeed sexualisation, are all too often abstracted from these material power inequities (Coy and Garner 2012; Gill 2012).

Second, is the notion that using the body for profit is an indicator of women's empowerment and sexual autonomy (Gill 2007; Coy and Garner 2010). Many elements of sexualised popular culture have seeped across from the sex industry, for example, pole dancing classes marketed as fitness; lap dancing as normative corporate entertainment; pimping as a verb in everyday language (Coy, Wakeling and Garner 2011). All imply or involve the exchange value of a female body that is most prized when youthful and conforming to racially delineated aesthetics. Sexualised popular culture is not simply the mainstreaming of sex, but of commercial sex (Boyle 2010): of similar values that underpin the global sex industry – men's entitlement to the consumption of women's bodies for sexual release and the notion that women are empowered by capitalising on their bodies for personal gain. Gender is also only one axis of inequality here; intersections with race and ethnicity are evident in framings of young black women as hypersexualised and black men as predatory (End Violence Against Women 2011a; Gill 2012).

This is an important point as feminist critical analyses of sexualisation are often traduced as attempts to repress expressions of sexuality. However, these critiques are not rooted in fear or disapproval of sexual expression, but of how this sexual expression is constructed, reinforcing gender and race as social hierarchies in which men are afforded greater social, economic and cultural capital and respect. If sexualised popular culture is understood not as a manifestation of sexual liberation but instead as a means of reinstating unequal gender norms (Dines 2011; McRobbie 2009; Walby 2011), then it becomes an issue for all those concerned with achieving gender equality and social justice. It is for this reason that Rosalind Gill (2011) suggests that perhaps we should be referring to 'sexist' rather than 'sexualised' popular culture, and exploring intersections with race/ethnicity. To date, policy responses to, and academic perspectives on, sexualisation have somewhat patchily focused on gender and sexism, but paid minimal attention to how they might be shaped by race/ethnicity and class.

REFLECTIONS ON POLICY FRAMEWORKS AND ACADEMIC PERSPECTIVES

The policy trajectory on sexualisation in England and Wales can be seen as, 'from child protection to violence against women…and back again' (Coy and Garner 2012, p.289). An initial review of safety and wellbeing in the digital world (Byron, 2008) preceded a specific exploration of sexualisation commissioned by the Home Office as part of their strategy addressing violence against women. This review (Papadopoulos 2010) took an explicitly gendered approach from the outset, and explored existing research on links between exposure to sexualised material (including pornography) and attitudes to violence against women. The key conclusion was that sexualised media reinforces heteronormative gender stereotyping by portraying women and girls to be sexually desirable and equating masculine sexuality with conquest. In other words, the review concluded that sexualised popular culture forms a 'conducive context' (Kelly 2007) for violence against women and girls. This concept refers to how combinations of social narratives and locations normalise certain practices – for example, that representation of women and girls embracing sexual display coalesce with those of predatory masculinity to corrode young women's ability to resist sexual pressure (Coy 2009; End Violence Against Women 2011a). In no small part this conclusion reflected that the review team consulted widely with women's organisations that drew on their practice-based evidence of working directly with young women (and for some, also young men) and recognised that how young people perceive 'doing' gender profoundly influences how they negotiate sexual encounters and relationships.

For instance, women's organisations can provide multiple, diverse examples where young women link their experiences of sexual violence/harassment/exploitation with the messages from sexualised popular culture (Coy and Garner 2012). These examples relate to behaviours that appear to young people as normalised through their very ubiquity: specific forms of sexual invasion of young women's bodies that reflect recent music videos, and notions of women and girls as possessions/commodities that are expressed through the language of 'pimping'. It is too simplistic to suggest that young people are passively mimicking actions they absorb from media; what matters is the extent to which these chime with dominant social mores and thus appear naturalised (Gill 2012). In an evaluation of a school-based prevention programme on sexual exploitation, one of the themes articulated by young men about messages in sexualised media was a link with masculinity – 'it's what boys do' (cited in Coy, Thiara and Kelly 2011; see also End Violence Against Women 2011b). Attempts in the Papadopoulos review to unpick how popular culture might reflect and reproduce gendered social norms also fit with obligations under international human rights conventions – the 1979 Convention of the Elimination of All Forms of Discrimination Against Women (CEDAW) and the 1995 Beijing Platform for Action – to address stereotyped sexualised representations of women in the media (UN 2006; Papadopoulos 2010).

Yet despite this progressive approach to gender equality, the Papadopoulos review also legitimised sexualisation by defining it in terms of 'adult sexuality', which young people will one day be ready to 'deal with' (Papadopoulos 2010, p.23). The concern here appears to be at what stage in the life course young people 'should' enter the sexualised cultural landscape rather than the sexualised cultural landscape itself (Coy and Garner 2012).

A change of administration in 2010 brought another review, conducted by the Chief Executive of the Mothers' Union (Bailey 2011). While also notionally linked to the Conservative–Liberal Democrat Coalition Government's violence against women strategy, the Bailey review marked a discernible shift in emphasis towards defining the 'problem' of sexualised popular culture solely as a matter of age-appropriate engagement. There are token references to the significance of gender in terms of stereotyping in clothes and toys, but the core of the review is the threat to childhood posed by sexualisation. This framing is reflected in the recommendations, which centre on age restrictions on sexualised imagery and material and ensuring that advertising and various forms of media (notably television and music videos) are 'family-friendly' (see Bailey 2011).

Alongside policy reviews, an extensive body of scholarship has developed. Academic debate on sexualisation is a hydra with many heads: anthropologists, sociologists, psychologists, educationalists, cultural studies scholars have all contributed to conceptual development and empirical research. Undoubtedly, understandings of the possible issues at stake have been enriched by these multiple perspectives, the piquancy of dialogue they produce, and thoughtful explorations of the definitions and discourses in play. For the most part, though, academic research and theory has focused on how sexualisation influences self-image, notions of empowerment and agency, and neglected how these messages might be related to young people's sexual practices (Coy and Garner 2012).

The missing piece of the jigsaw in both policy and academia is a gendered analysis that takes in not just femininity but also masculinity (for an exception, see Garner 2012). How young women 'do' femininity, the ways in which they are able to engage with or resist dominant codes and constructions are profoundly relational. The extent to which (young) women are able to act with a sense of autonomy is shaped – and for many, restricted – by how (young) men assert their greater sense of entitlement to sex.

Research on 'sexting' between young people illustrates this acutely. A recent exploratory study suggests that the sending and receiving of sexual images reflects the, 'total normalisation of sexualised communications and imagery that young people are receiving and negotiating in their day to day lives at school and beyond' (Ringrose et al. 2012, p.39). The significance of gender is clear and present; girls are significantly more likely to be the object of 'sexts', which are also frequently non-consensual. Young people's engagement with technology and social media is integral here, facilitating new means by which young women are abused and harassed (Funnell 2011; Ringrose et al. 2012). Ringrose et al. conclude that the practice of sexting reflects heteronormative notions where doing 'boy' involves sexually invading young women's personal space and bodies, and call for further investigation of boys and masculinity (Ringrose et al. 2012). Yet connections between sexualised popular culture and sexual practices, and willingness to problematise hegemonic masculinity, are absent from much debate, particularly in popular discourse.

CONTRADICTIONS AND CONFUSIONS: SEXUALISATION IN POPULAR DISCOURSE

The role of the media with respect to sexualisation is complicated, not least because it is a source of sexualised imagery and discourse, and of critique and concern about such images and messages (see Gill 2012 for an extended discussion). In the outraged populist froth about sexualised popular culture, there are two ways in which contradictions and confusions are evident. The first is an explicit hypocrisy, which heaps opprobrium on images and products that present a 'danger' to children despite having built a core income from sexually objectifying (young) women. For instance, in 2010 *The Sun* newspaper, (in)famous for a daily photograph of a semi-naked young woman on Page 3, waged a campaign against the sale of padded bikinis for girls, resulting in their withdrawal from major supermarkets and high street shops. With headlines such as 'Paedo heaven on our high street' (Hamilton 2010a) and 'Paedo bikini banned' (Hamilton 2010b), *The Sun* embraces the notion that children (girls) are endangered by sexualised clothing, yet remains obstinately impervious to their own role in eroticising young female bodies.

The *Daily Mail* has been similarly singled out for the tension between their incendiary crusade against the sexualisation of children, while simultaneously running stories on their website Mail Online – with an average of 100 million unique readers per month (Press Gazette 2012) – which comment lasciviously on young women's breasts, bodies and bikinis (Gill 2012; Robbins 2012). In September 2012, tabloid newspapers condemned toddler 'beauty pageants' yet published large photographs of young girls in bikinis and makeup underneath headlines that made sexual allusions to 'cavorting provocatively' (Eaves *et al.* 2012). Women's organisations that gave evidence to the recent Leveson Inquiry into the culture and ethics of the media highlighted examples of this incongruity (End Violence Against Women 2012; Object 2012). Lord Justice Leveson's final report called attention to:

> the unfortunate juxtaposition of the article expressing outrage at a satirical programme on paedophilia and an article commenting on a 15 year-old's breasts exposes a hypocrisy in relation to the sexualisation of young girls and women that is seen beyond the Page 3 tabloids: some have commented on the awkward co-existence of the Daily Mail's support for 'traditional values' with the Mail Online's 'sidebar of shame'. (Leveson 2012, pp.663–634)

The second approach is more confused than contradictory, a perhaps less consciously paradoxical framing, yet also focuses on the 'developmental assumptions' of sexualised popular culture as if there were little or no impact for adult women (Gill 2012). For example, the 'Let Girls be Girls' campaign launched in 2010 by Mumsnet identifies the perils of clothing, toys and marketing that catapult girls into adult sexual mores. Here, the ways in which sexualisation is profoundly gendered are acknowledged, as are the impacts for adult women, but the focus is on making a difference for the next generation of girls (Mumsnet no date). The Channel 4 campaign 'Stop Pimping Our Kids' explicitly draws a developmental line in the sand, by defending the use of sexualised imagery in lads' mags as their 'selling point', which is only problematic when stocked at 'children's eye level' (Channel 4 no date).

Thus the only available critique of sexualisation within media and popular discourse centres on preserving children's innocence (Coy and Garner 2012). As noted earlier, current policy has enthusiastically taken up and built on this approach. The Bailey review (2011) recommended a code of practice for retailers, which proscribes 'scaled-down' sexualised products for children, ducking the need to interrogate the pressures on adult women to conform with a sexualised presentation of self. Another recommendation proposes restricting advertisements featuring sexualised imagery near schools (Bailey 2011). This can, however, only be a symbolic measure. Children and young people not only encounter such advertisements – which have been described as a visual form of sexual harassment (Rosewarne 2007) – on their way to and from school. Almost all engagement with public space is likely to involve viewing advertisements on billboards, buses and shop displays that feature women's bodies in sexualised poses. Significant proportions of young people are exposed to sexual and pornographic material online (see Ringrose *et al.* 2012 for an overview). Furthermore, as feminist campaign organisation Object (2012) trenchantly point out, tabloid newspapers that feature women in sexual display are regularly sold at children's eye level.

What underpins this incoherent approach is an unwillingness to face fundamental questions about ongoing gender inequalities. In the next and final section I outline ways to engage young people in these questions.

INTEGRATING A GENDERED ANALYSIS INTO CONVERSATION WITH YOUNG PEOPLE

Addressing the potential harms of sexualisation – social and individual – requires an approach rooted in children's rights and protection and gender equality (End Violence Against Women 2011a). While it may be more complex for young people, with limited life experience and social autonomy, to negotiate messages transmitted in popular culture, adults are not suddenly self-assured and 'empowered' as they cross the threshold into their majority (Gill 2012). Therefore, both generation and gender are critically important. There are a number of potential ways in which discussion of their significance and meaning can be integrated into practice with young people.

First, talking about sexualised youth culture reinforces the notion that sexualised popular culture is itself not a problem, only the age at which young people engage with it. While many young people have specific relationships with music, fashion, television, film and indeed digital technology, they do not inhabit an entirely separate cultural field from adults. Limiting discussions to the term – and concept – 'youth culture' thus seals the doors on interrogating wider social contexts.

A common recommendation is for young people to participate in media literacy sessions, equipping them with skills to decode the messages they see and expose their artifice. This is a welcome start, and has a vital place in enabling young people to think critically about sexualised media. However, as Gill (2012) has argued, to view media literacy as an 'inoculation' against harmful or negative influences assumes that their newly acquired critical skills will cancel out any other responses. It also places all responsibility for change on young people, rather than seeking to transform popular culture itself.

Notwithstanding the urgency of social change, in the here and now, perhaps one means of enabling young people to explore a range of responses – which may also transform future unequal relations and hierarchies between women and men – is to ensure that fundamental questions about gender are at the heart of conversations with young people. The need for Sex and Relationships Education (SRE), or its equivalents, to address 'doing' gender and conducive contexts for violence against women and girls has long been noted (see Coy *et al.* 2010). Pressures related to sexualisation should form a central theme here (Ringrose *et al.* 2012). As not all children and young people are in regular education, these conversations need to be taking place in all youth settings.

Recognising popular culture as a site where unequal gender norms are reinstated (McRobbie 2009), and as a conducive context for violence against women and girls, means that we can, and should, engage young people in the often overlooked yet important question: how do gendered representations in sexualised popular culture provide templates for what it means to be a boy/man, girl/woman? For example, what do they make of images that consistently show women and girls semi-naked while men are fully clothed? How do they understand personal and social power – the 'relationship (if any) between subjective feelings of empowerment and actually being empowered' (Gill 2012, p.737)? What meanings, if any, do they attribute to forms of commercial sex that have become normalised leisure activities? How are all these reflected in their understandings of gendered codes for sexual behaviour? How do they view and interpret intersections of race and gender in sexualised imagery and discourse? Finally, and perhaps most significantly, how do they negotiate sexual consent and coercion according to what they understand of 'doing gender'?

CONCLUSION

'Feminism [is] an unfinished project – not only for young people, but for all of us' (Gill 2012 p.743).

Addressing sexualisation only in terms of generation without gender is a limited approach. Yet current popular and policy debates around sexualisation centre on the idea that contemporary popular culture prematurely imposes 'sexuality' on children before they are ready to deal with it. What is necessary is a reframing of the question to be about the impact of sexualisation for women and girls; for men and boys and how they make sense of it and act in relation to it; to ask how sexualisation perpetuates stereotypes about masculinity and femininity. This then leads us to conversations about how gendered representations across forms of sexualised popular culture form a 'conducive context' (Kelly 2007) for violence against women and girls (Coy 2009;

End Violence Against Women 2011a). Women's organisations that support survivors of sexual violence and carry out prevention work in schools around issues of sexual consent see in sexualised popular culture the same messages about gender that underpin the dynamics of violence and abuse. Approaches that ignore the significance of gender fail to account for this.

The current emphasis on addressing sexualisation is to achieve a 'family-friendly' society (Bailey 2011). If we reframe this as 'woman-friendly', we move closer to tackling the gendered hierarchies reinforced in and through sexualised popular culture, and thus ground our interactions with young people in the realities of their present and future everyday lives.

REFERENCES

Bailey, R. (2011) *Letting Children Be Children: Report of an Independent Review of the Commercialisation and Sexualisation of Childhood.* London: Department for Education.

Boyle, K. (2010) 'Introduction: Everyday Pornography.' In K. Boyle (ed.) *Everyday Pornography.* London: Routledge.

Byron, T. (2008) *Safer Children in a Digital World: The Report of the Byron Review.* London: Department for Children, Schools and Families/Department for Culture, Media and Sport.

Channel 4 (no date) 'Stop Pimping Our Kids!' Available at: http://sexperienceuk. channel4.com/stop-pimping-our-kids, accessed on 12 February 2013.

Coy, M. (2009) 'Milkshakes, lady lumps and growing up to want boobies: how the sexualisation of popular culture limits girls' horizons.' *Child Abuse Review, 18,* 6, 372–383.

Coy, M. and Garner, M. (2010) 'Glamour modelling and the marketing of self-sexualisation: critical reflections.' *International Journal of Cultural Studies, 13,* 6, 657–675.

Coy, M. and Garner, M. (2012) 'Definitions, discourses and dilemmas: policy and academic engagement with the sexualisation of popular culture.' *Gender and Education, 24,* 3, 285–301.

Coy, M., Thiara, R. and Kelly., L. (2011) *Boys Think Girls are Toys? An Evaluation of the Nia Project Sexual Exploitation Prevention Programme.* London: Child and Woman Abuse Studies Unit, London Metropolitan University.

Coy, M., Lee, K., Roach, C. and Kelly, L. (2010) *A Missing Link? An Exploratory Study of Connections between Teenage Pregnancy and Non-Consensual Sex.* London: Child and Woman Abuse Studies Unit, London Metropolitan University.

Coy, M., Wakeling, J., and Garner, M. (2011) 'Selling sex sells: representations of prostitution and the sex industry in sexualised popular culture as symbolic violence.' *Women's Studies International Forum, 34*, 441–448.

Dines, G. (2011) 'The New Lolita: Pornography and the Sexualization of Childhood.' In M. Tankard Reist and A. Bray (eds) *Big Porn Inc: Exposing the Harms of the Global Pornography Industry.* Melbourne: Spinifex Press.

Eaves, End Violence Against Women (EVAW) (2012) 'Equality Now and Object.' *Just the Women.* London: EVAW. Available at www.endviolenceagainstwomen. org.uk/data/files/resources/51/Just-the-Women-Nov-2012.pdf, accessed on 28 April 2013.

End Violence Against Women (2011a) *A Different World is Possible: A Call for Long-term and Targeted Action to Prevent Violence Against Women and Girls.* London: End Violence Against Women.

End Violence Against Women (2011b) *A Different World is Possible: Promising Practices to Prevent Violence Against Women and Girls.* London: End Violence Against Women.

End Violence Against Women (2012) *EVAW Coalition Submission to the Leveson Inquiry.* London: End Violence Against Women. Available at www. endviolenceagainstwomen.org.uk/resources/43/evaw-coalition-submission-to-the-leveson-inquiry-jan-2012, accessed on 28 April 2013.

Fawcett Society (2013) *Sex and Power 2013: Who runs Britain?* London: Fawcett Society. Available at: http://www.fawcettsociety.org.uk/wp-content/uploads/2013/02/Sex-and-Power-2013-FINAL-REPORT.pdf, accessed on 1 March 2013.

Funnell, N. (2011) 'Sexting and Peer-to-peer Porn.' In M. Tankard Reist and A. Bray (eds) *Big Porn Inc: Exposing the Harms of the Global Pornography Industry.* Melbourne: Spinifex Press.

Garner, M. (2012) 'The missing link: the sexualisation of culture and men.' *Gender and Education, 24,* 3, 325–331.

Gill, R. (2007) 'Postfeminist media culture: elements of a sensibility.' *European Journal of Cultural Studies, 10,* 2, 147–166.

Gill, R. (2011) 'Sexism reloaded, or, it's time to get angry again!' *Feminist Media Studies, 11,* 1, 61–71.

Gill, R. (2012) 'Media, empowerment and the "sexualization of culture" debates.' *Sex Roles, 66,* 11/12, 736–745.

Hamilton, J. (2010a) 'Paedo heaven on our high street.' *The Sun,* 15 April.

Hamilton, J. (2010b) 'Paedo bikini banned.' *The Sun,* 14 April.

Kelly, L. (2007) 'A Conducive Context: Trafficking of Persons in Central Asia.' In M. Lee (ed.) *Human Trafficking.* Cullompton: Willan Publishing.

Leveson, B. (2012) *An Inquiry into the Culture, Practices and Ethics of the Press: Report [Leveson].* Volume 2. London: The Stationery Office.

McRobbie, A. (2008) 'Pornographic permutations.' *Communications, 11,* 3, 225–236.

Mumsnet (no date) 'Let Girls Be Girls campaign.' Available at: http://www.mumsnet.com/campaigns/let-girls-be-girls, accessed on 12 February 2013.

McRobbie, A. (2009) *The Aftermath of Feminism: Gender, Culture and Social Change.* London: Sage Publications.

Papadopoulos, L. (2010) *Sexualisation of Young People Review.* London: Home Office.

Press Gazette (2012) 'Mail Online surges past 100m browsers in August.' *Press Gazette.* Available at www.pressgazette.co.uk/mail-online-surges-past-100m-browsers-august, accessed on 28 April 2013.

Object (2012) *Leveson Inquiry: Witness Statement of OBJECT.* Available at www.object.org.uk/files/Witness%20statement%20for%20the%20website.pdf, accessed on 28 April 2013.

Office for National Statistics (2012) *Annual Survey of Hours and Earnings, 2012 Provisional Results.* London: ONS. Available at: http://www.ons.gov.uk/ons/dcp171778_286243.pdf, accessed on 4 January 2013.

Ringrose, J., Gill, R., Livingstone, S. and Harvey, L. (2012) *A Qualitative Study of Children, Young People and 'Sexting'.* London: NSPCC.

Robbins, M. (2012) 'Sex, children and Mail Online.' *New Statesman,* 11 June. Available at www.newstatesman.com/blogs/voices/2012/06/sex-children-and-mail-online, accessed on 28 April 2013.

Rosewarne, L. (2007) 'Pin-ups in public space: sexist outdoor advertising as sexual harassment.' *Women's Studies International Forum, 30,* 4, 313–325.

United Nations (2006) *Secretary-General's in-depth study on violence against women* A/61/122/Add.1. Available at: http://daccessdds.un.org/doc/UNDOC/GEN/N06/419/74/PDF/N0641974.pdf, accessed on 2 January, 2013.

Walby, S. (2011) *The Future of Feminism.* Cambridge: Polity Press.

Whelehan, I. (2000) *Overloaded: Popular Culture and the Future of Feminism.* London: Women's Press.

PART 3

FIGHTING BACK AGAINST COMMERCIAL AND SEXUAL EXPLOITATION

CHAPTER 12

HELPING CHILDREN TO STAND UP TO SOCIETY

CRITICAL CHALLENGES AND CULTURE JAMMING

PROFESSOR STEPHEN D. BROOKFIELD

When we think of child protection we often focus on physical violence, sexual abuse, and bullying. The perpetrators are usually identifiable in the child's family, social network, or peer group. More recently, attention has been focused on cyber-bullying in which a group makes someone the subject of ridicule in online forums by posting lies designed to humiliate the target. This chapter looks at a different, often more subtle form of abuse – ideological abuse. By ideological abuse I mean subjecting children to a sustained battery of images, practices, and messages that encourage an unquestioning acceptance of dominant ideologies such as capitalism, militarism, patriarchy, White supremacy, and heterosexism. Educationally, one of the few recourses we have to combat this abuse is to teach children to think critically in ways that will help them counter and challenge these ideologies. In this chapter I examine the elements of critical thinking and explore ways to teach it.

In June 2012 the Texan Republican Party created a stir amongst educators in the USA by adopting an official party platform in which they, "oppose the teaching of Higher Order Thinking Skills (HOTS) (values clarification), critical thinking skills (that) have the purpose of challenging the student's fixed beliefs and undermining parental authority" (Republican Party of Texas 2012, p.12). By way of contrast, the UK Department for Education articulated governmental support for teaching critical thinking to children (Department for Education 2008) regarding it as a way of combating extremism and increasing political participation (Bonnell *et al.* 2011). Predictably, liberals and progressives in the USA had a field day railing against the Texan platform, but one thing that can be said for it is that it captures how many children and adolescents experience critical thinking exercises when they are first introduced. Teachers, youth workers, and parents who initiate a process of asking children and young adults to clarify the assumptions that inform their thinking and actions, or who invite them to be open to perspectives that they had not considered before, both upset and challenge them. So push back, avoidance, and resistance is certain.

I begin this chapter by exploring exactly what constitutes the process of critical thinking that Texan Republicans so detest. I then situate teaching critical thinking in the context of models of child and adolescent cognitive development. The rest of the chapter addresses how critical thinking can be cultivated in the face of enormous and sustained ideological manipulation, particularly militarism and capitalism. Cultivating is an appropriate gerund to use, since so much teaching and modeling for critical thinking takes the form of preparing the ground for future intellectual growth. Additionally, the direction and amount of growth itself is affected by the continued nurturance and care the plant receives.

HUNTING ASSUMPTIONS: THE CORE OF CRITICAL THINKING

Different intellectual traditions (analytic philosophy, natural science, pragmatism, and so on) define critical thinking in different ways. In this chapter I draw primarily on the critical theory tradition in which criticality is equated with being able to uncover power and ideological manipulation. This involves becoming aware of assumptions one has accepted about how power is being exercised on you by others, what are abusive and ethical uses of power you enact yourself, and what constitutes empowerment. Critical thinking *à* la critical theory scrutinizes these assumptions and asks questions such as when does dominant power manipulate me? What's a justifiable exercise of power? How does empowerment work?

The core process in all critical thinking is hunting assumptions. Trying to discover what our assumptions are, and then trying to judge when, and how far, these are accurate, is something that happens every time critical thinking occurs. You cannot think critically without hunting assumptions; that is, without trying to uncover assumptions and then trying to assess their accuracy and validity—their fit with life.

Assumptions are guides to truth embedded in our mental outlooks. They are the daily rules that frame how we make decisions and take actions. Everyday communications are subject to a continuous and ever-present set of assumptions. We make assumptions about the meaning behind the words we, and others, use, about the meaning of certain gestures, expressions or pauses, or about how to respond to a comment. Assumptions inform our judgments about whether or not someone is telling the truth, or how to recognize when we are being manipulated.

As we move through each hour of each day our actions are always based in assumptions, most of which have been confirmed by repeated experience. I brush my teeth assuming that doing so will prevent tooth decay and cut down on the expense and pain of dental procedures. I choose my food for the day based on assumptions about how healthy, or how pleasurable, eating those foods will be. I set the thermostat and choose clothes based on assumptions I'm making drawn from the weather report. As I drive to an appointment I lock the back door, fill the petrol tank, follow traffic lights, and rely on street signs or the sat-nav on the assumption that doing all these things will get me where I want to go in the speediest and safest way possible. All the assumptions I've mentioned are held because experience has shown them to be accurate.

Assumptions as instinctive guides to truth operate at much deeper levels than that of daily routine, however. Many are linked to dominant ideologies such as capitalism, patriarchy, or heterosexism, and what critical theorists call the instrumentalization of reason (Brookfield 2005). This is a fearsome sounding piece of academic jargon that actually is pretty easy to understand. Instrumentalized reasoning is described by Horkheimer and Adorno (1972) and

Marcuse (1964) as the kind of thinking that is most valued in contemporary life. Basically, you reason instrumentally whenever you try to fix a problem without ever questioning whether or not the problem is the one that needs fixing. You reason instrumentally when you tinker with a system—for example, how to assess whether students are learning correctly—so as to improve it, to make it more effective. You don't ask whose interests are served by solving the problem, because you're so focused on being a good "fix-it" kind of person.

When people think critically they question the fundamental assumptions behind how problems are defined. They ask the big questions of life – what constitutes learning? How do we organize organizations and communities to encourage compassion or fairness? What is the fundamental purpose of teaching? What does it mean to work authentically? Needless to say, in an instrumentalized culture asking these questions is usually seen as either utopian, impractical, or idealistic, something we are expected to grow out of and to regard as an annoying waste of time.

IDEOLOGICAL ASSUMPTIONS

Assumptions that spring from dominant ideologies are particularly hard to uncover, precisely because these ideologies are everywhere, so common as to be thought blindingly obvious and therefore not worthy of being the object of sustained questioning. Ideologies are the sets of beliefs and practices that are accepted by the majority as common-sense ways of organizing the world. Some of them operate at macro-levels, such as the democratic assumption that majority vote is the decision-making system that most fairly meets the most important needs of the majority. Others operate at micro-levels, such as the meritocratic assumption that a teacher, department head, or community leader occupies their position because their abilities and experiences have caused them to rise to that level.

Capitalism and democracy are two dominant ideologies that are highly public. Children learn them in school, from the media, in their families, and through the organizations of civil society such as the church or local political associations. Much harder to identify but equally influential are ideologies that are more submerged, such as White supremacy, militarism, patriarchy, or heterosexism. These ideologies all hold that leadership is best exercised by Whites and males and heterosexuals, because these are deemed to be smarter, more emotionally stable, and more accomplished, and that in settling disputes the use of force is the most effective instrumental shortcut. Legislation has ensured that these beliefs are spoken mostly in private, off the record, or off the air.

Ideology is learned not just through the spoken or written word, but also through behavior (what critical theorists call practices). When we go through life seeing leadership positions filled by Whites, particularly White men, and when no one remarks on this fact, we are learning dominant ideology. When a person of color, or a woman, or an 'out' Gay or Lesbian attains a position of prominence or influence, and this fact is highlighted as an example of democracy and liberty in action, dominant ideology is also, somewhat perversely, in action. After all, when a heterosexual White male attains the some position, his race, gender or sexuality is rarely mentioned. This is because Whiteness, maleness and heterosexuality are the leadership norms that we observe everywhere and that we internalize without being aware of it. Paradoxically, an event that seems to disrupt and challenge dominant ideology—such as the election of a bi-racial President, or the appointment of an African-American woman as Secretary of State—actually confirms it, at least in the short term. The very fact that these are exceptions, and celebrated as such, actually confirms the enduring influence of the norm.

LEARNING HEGEMONY

One other facet in learning to think critically is important to clarify. When we think critically we are sometimes helped to realize that the actions and beliefs we think are in our best interests are actually harmful to us, even when we're not aware of that fact. This is how I connect the concept of hegemony (drawn from critical theory) to critical thinking. Hegemony is in place when people behave in ways that they think are good for them, not realizing that they are being harmed and colluding in their own misery. People suffering from anorexia assume that by not eating they make themselves more beautiful and less unsightly, closer to the idealized body images they see in advertising. People who assume that good workers need to be available 24/7 to serve the ends of their employers think ill health and exhaustion are natural.

So part of critical thinking is making sure that the actions that flow from our assumptions are justifiable according to some notion of goodness or desirability. This is where things start to get complicated, and where questions of power arise. What if you and I disagree about the right response to a situation? How do we decide which is the better, more critical response? For example, if I think capitalism rewards those who already have and secures permanent inequity, and you think it ensures that the spirit of individual entrepreneurship stays vigorous and therefore is essential for the functioning of a healthy democracy, how do we assess who is thinking more correctly? Each of us can cite evidence, scan experience, and produce credible, authoritative individuals who support our respective point of view. But ultimately, each of us has arrived at our position from a mixture of analyzing our experiences, thinking in the most critical way we can about them, and then allying our analysis with our vision of what the world looks like when it's working properly.

Critical thinking can't be analyzed as a discrete process of mental actions that can be separated from our object of analysis, from exactly what it is that we're thinking critically about. If critical thinking is understood only as a process of analyzing information so we can take actions that produce desired results, then some of the most vicious acts of human behavior could be defined as critical thinking. Serial killers presumably analyze how best to take steps to avoid detection by examining their assumptions about how to stalk victims, hide evidence, and dispose of bodies. Religious cult leaders think critically about how to disassociate new recruits from their past lives and allegiances, and how then to create an identification with the new leader. Spousal abusers can think critically about how to beat up a partner in a way that hides bruises and overt signs of injury, whilst making that partner feel that they deserved the abuse and that the abuser was doing it for their own good.

CRITICAL THINKING IN CHILDREN AND YOUNG ADULTS

Between the project of encouraging critical thinking in children and young people, and the reality of helping people push back against commercial exploitation and ideological manipulation, lies the complex territory of cognitive development. The developmental framework of Piaget, so influential in cognitive development theory (Bjorklund 2011; Charlesworth 2008), places the capacity for logical reasoning as typically beginning around age seven and lasting until age 12. During this period of concrete operations, children are purported to engage in decision-making during which they make choices on the basis of reviewing past experience.

The period of formal operations coincides roughly with adolescence, and during this period decision-making becomes more complex as young people manage multiple variables and become more aware of context. An interesting example of this is in the first series of *The Wire*, the TV show that focuses strongly on the adolescent and pre-adolescent world of Baltimore drug dealers. In one scene Wallace, a teenage drug dealer, is helping his younger brother do a math homework problem involving a bus that picks up and drops off passengers at different stops. The brother can't get the right answer so Wallace reframes the problem in terms of selling drug vials. His brother immediately gets the correct answer and Wallace, in frustration, asks how he can compute that problem correctly when it involves selling vials, but answers the question wrongly when the problem involves passengers on a bus. His brother simply replies, "Count be wrong—they'll fuck you up." Context is all—getting the calculation right on the street is a matter of life and death; in the classroom, totally irrelevant.

A body of work has recently built on Piaget's ideas to propose a stage of post-formal operations (Sinnott 2009) in which young adults start to adapt logical patterns of reasoning to particular contexts. Basseches (2005) argues that young adults are able to start thinking dialectically; that is, to be able to hold in congenial tension two ideas that seem to be diametrically opposed, but that are both true depending on context. So, for example, someone can believe as a general rule that one should be open, honest, and transparent in building relationships, but be capable of lying and manipulation when a particular situation calls for it. An adult at a post-formal stage has no trouble believing that either behavior is justified depending on context. An adolescent in a formal stage of cognitive development, however, will have great difficulty in accepting that both contradictory ways of behaving are appropriate depending on the situation.

These are all hypothetical formulations and it would be foolish to generalize all Piagetian models to children of every race, class, gender, and culture at every stage in human history! But this body of work does give those of us who work with children and young people some useful pointers. First, it helps us keep in realistic perspective what it is reasonable to expect. In early stages of childhood, the giving of reasons represents the major conceptual bridge children cross. The ability to provide evidence for these reasons represents the second conceptual Rubicon of early adolescence, together with a developing ability to judge its validity.

THINKING CRITICALLY ABOUT MILITARISM

When it comes to helping young people think critically about dominant ideology, however, the experiential dimension of the stage of formal operations is crucial. Ideologies of capitalism, militarism, patriarchy, White supremacy, and heterosexism are most effectively challenged by experience, not by rational argument. When ideology effectively disseminates itself through media and the micro-reality of daily conversations, it usually takes a counter experience to prompt some critical questioning. In this regard, bullying is a potential starting point for the analysis of militarism. Children in the concrete operations stage are no strangers to bullying and the majority have either been victims of it, or onlookers witnessing it. But in the concrete operations stage the typical response is to internalize the slurs, beatings and critiques of others and to feel that these are both deserved and empirically accurate.

However, with the development of formal operations the possibility of recognizing that bullying is a generic social phenomenon starts to emerge. Through films (*Precious*, *Mean Girls*, *Bully*, *The Karate Kid*, *Reviving Ophelia*), TV shows (*Glee*, *Bullied*), fiction (Andreas 2011), or the web (www.stopbullying.gov; www.bullying.co.uk), adolescents can move beyond a purely personal interpretation or response to consider similarities existing in cases outside their own experience. Once generic dynamics begin to be noticed then the work of considering causation can begin. And then the process of tracing personal experiences back to ideological causes becomes possible, though intensely difficult.

I believe there is a connection between militarism as an ideology and bullying as an individually experienced manifestation of that ideology. For the last decade in the USA where I live there has been a relatively uncritical celebration of militarism, specifically of making the world safe from terrorism by fighting the "War on Terror." I left England in 1982, partly out of disgust for the incredibly jingoistic support of the Falklands War, and, with uncanny regularity, I have watched as the UK and USA have become embroiled in Middle East conflict every ten years or so. I should say, however, that I am not a pacifist. I believe that force sometimes needs to be met with force, and that war is sometimes justified. I come from a military family and my parents both met while serving in the Royal Navy. I think that in war we sometimes see the best of human qualities as well as the worst.

As an ideology, however, militarism glorifies the use of force for force's sake, believes the only way to change behavior or maintain order is through the deployment of force, justifies the murder, torture, and rape of civilians as "collateral damage," and emphasizes the constant stockpiling of weapons as the best way to secure peace. Women, the elderly, and children are typically the least defenseless against militarism, although what constitutes being a victim of militarism is complex. Child soldiers are clearly victims of this ideology even as they are enacters of it.

In a militarist ideology, "the question surrounding war and violence is not whether they will occur, but rather who will survive" (O'Neill and Sullivan 2002, p.174). In commenting on what can be learned from work on Mojab's (2010) work on women, war, and violence, Horsman (no date) documents the effects of living under militarism: the erosion of self-confidence, the development of feelings of blame and guilt people feel for their situations, depression, anxiety, post-traumatic stress syndrome (PTSD), and insomnia. Crucially, for learning, there is a fear of being punished or humiliated for making mistakes. Now, compare how the victims of school or neighborhood bullying talk about the way they internalize the blame for their own bullying—the anxiety, depression, insomnia, psychosomatic illnesses they endure—and a direct causal trajectory connects an individual instance of bullying to the ideology of militarism.

THINKING CRITICALLY ABOUT CONSUMERISM

For children and young people a crucial element in consumerism is commodity fetishism—the worship of consumer goods. In a commodified world people, "judge themselves by their own market value and learn what they are from what happens to them in the capitalist economy" (Horkheimer and Adorno 1972, p.211). People have become so seduced by the commodities produced by capitalism that their lives are geared to the pursuit of these and their self-worth is bound up with their possession of them. Identity is branded through the pursuit of branded, labeled goods, to the extent that children and adolescents can be mugged, or even murdered, for a particular branded jacket. Commodities (or consumer goods) thus become, "an ideological curtain behind which the real evil is concentrated" (Horkheimer and Adorno 1972, p.xv) as people are enslaved by the myth of economic success. Consequently, "life in the late capitalist era is a constant initiation rite. Everyone must show that he wholly identifies himself with the power which is belaboring him" (Horkheimer and Adorno, p.153).

In the post-Second World War era, Fromm proposed an analysis of capitalism that still rings remarkably true today. He argued that the market requires people who are malleable in the extreme to serve as consumers of its products. The more malleable consumers are, the better they are suited to capitalism. Ideally, global capitalism is best served by large populations that equate living with consuming, that gain their identities from the purchase of certain branded products, and that shy away from buying anything too idiosyncratic or locally produced. The greater the standardization of taste and consumption patterns across national boundaries, the more effectively production can be streamlined and commodities marketed. Thus, contemporary capitalism produces children and young people, "whose tastes are standardized and can be easily influenced and anticipated" (Fromm 1956, p.110). Such people like nothing better than to buy the latest computer game, support one of a handful of European football teams (complete with replica kit), and watch the latest film adaptation of a graphic novel, wearing similarly branded clothes and shoes, all the while knowing that across the world numerous others are simultaneously engaged in the same activity.

Under capitalism, "the market decides the value of these human qualities" with the result that "relations between human beings... assume the character of relations between things" (Fromm 1941, p.140). Humanity is diminished as qualities such as a person's energy, skill, personality, and creativity become objectified—assets to be sold on the market of interpersonal relations. Each person, "sells himself and feels himself to be a commodity" (Fromm 1941, p.140). Fromm writes that in contemporary America, "our whole culture is based on the appetite for buying, on the idea of a mutually favorable exchange" (1956, p.3).

Fromm's extension of commodity fetishism into an analysis of rampant consumerism is still accurate half a century after it appeared. These days, contemporary commodity fetishism becomes evident not just in external apparel, but in the actual bodies of children. Girls in particular are bombarded by body images that emphasize slim bodies with large breasts. The body now becomes a commodity, one that can be shaped through anorexia, bulimia, or breast implants into a desirable package. Not only is one's personality—outgoing, extroverted, what the TV sitcom *How I Met Your Mother* calls a party animal "woo girl"—now seen as a marketable commodity, but one's body becomes an object. Self-worth is linked to body type and personality all contained within one marketable body/personality package.

CULTURE JAMMING

What kind of push back works best to challenge the hold of capitalist ideology on young minds? One creative approach takes place in shopping centers through the kinds of "culture jamming" that occur when activists and educators insert themselves into real-life cultural events and try to disrupt the expectations and behaviors of those involved. One of the most dramatic, energizing, and humorous jamming disruptions is the Reverend Billy's Church of the Stop Shopping. Reverend Billy (Bill Talen) stages "retail interventions" in shopping malls and retail stores in the form of church services accompanied with the Stop Shopping Gospel Choir. His troupe performs collective exorcisms, hears public confessions of congregation members' shopping addictions, and honors new Saints. He also authors guides to retail interventions such as the "Starbucks Invasion Kit".

In her description of Reverend Billy's work, Sandlin (2007) describes his intervention at a Disney store in which members of his "Church" carried crosses with Mickey and Minnie Mouse crucified on them. Sandlin quotes Billy as saying:

The Disney Company is the high church of retail. And that's why we put Mickey Mouse on the cross. We're taking two great organized religions [Christianity and what he calls the "Church of Consumerism"] and grinding them together and trying to confuse people so they can think in a new way. (Sandlin 2007, p.543)

In Sandlin's (2007) view, "the cultural resistance that occurs as an educational strategy within Reverend Billy's movement by its very nature addresses power and seeks change" (p.544).

Another real-life "field" experience that follows the logic of culture jamming is designed to demonstrate the superficiality of branding and deconstruct its power. Here you ask children to visit a charity shop and buy a cheaply priced garment that has a desirable brand label on it. The size of the garment is unimportant because in effect you're buying just the label. Then, you ask those same children to go to a supermarket to buy a generic, unlabeled item. Children take a piece of generic clothing home with them (for example, a pair of jeans or T-shirt) as well as the charity shop branded item. They, or you, then transfer the designer label on to the generic, brand-less item. At school the next day they wear their newly branded items and students take turns to try and guess which items worn by their peers are the genuine article and which have been artificially branded.

I did this exercise many times with my own children as they were growing up as a way of teaching them to counter sustained ideological abuse. Effectively it de-fetishized designer garments by recasting them as simple pieces of fabric on which a particular label had been fastened, rather than as semi-magical objects holding the power to bestow coolness on their wearers. I remember showing my children (who are both English as well as American), "Here's how we make an England football shirt." We would repeat the process described above but replay it using generic football jerseys and Umbro items bought from a charity shop. Instead of paying astronomical prices for Umbro's replica kit, we ended up paying pennies for an article that, to the naked eye, looked just the same. This was a deliberate attempt to de-couple them from the ideologically abusive belief that self-worth and desirability are tied to external designer trappings, and also to show them the obscene profit margins Nike, Adidas, Umbro and Puma operate under.

CONCLUSION

To break through ideological manipulation and help children and young people become critically aware of how their daily decisions and actions are connected to an unchallenged dominant ideology is enormously complex. It requires a skillful use of mass media, social media, and popular culture, together with interventions at the sites (for example, shopping centers) where ideology is enacted.

REFERENCES

Andreas, P. (2011) *Blue Car Racer*. Seattle, WA: CreateSpace Publishing.

Basseches, M. (2005) 'The development of dialectical thinking as an approach to integration.' *Integral Review, 1*, 47–63.

Bjorklund, D. (2011) *Children's Thinking: Cognitive Development and Individual Differences* (5th edition). Belmont, CA: Wadsworth.

Bonnell, J., Copestake, P., Kerr, D., Passy, R. *et al.* (2011) *Teaching Approaches that Help to Build Resilience to Extremism Among Young People*. Research Report DFE-RR119. London: Department for Education, Office for Public Management and National Foundation for Educational Research. Available at www.education.gov.uk/publications/eOrderingDownload/DFE-RR119. pdf, accessed on 29 April 2013.

Brookfield, S.D. (2005) *The Power of Critical Theory for Adult Learning and Teaching*. Milton Keynes: Open University Press/McGraw Hill.

Charlesworth, R. (2008) *Understanding Child Development* (8th edition). Belmont, CA: Wadsworth.

Department for Education (2008) *Working Together: Listening to the Voices of Children and Young People.* London: Department for Education. Available at www.education.gov.uk/publications/eOrderingDownload/DCSF-00410-2008.pdf, accessed on 29 April 2013.

Fromm, E. (1941) *Escape from Freedom.* New York: Holt, Rinehart and Winston.

Fromm, E. (1956) *The Sane Society.* London: Routledge, Kegan & Paul.

Horkheimer, M. and Adorno, T. (1972) *Dialectic of Enlightenment.* New York: Seabury Press.

Horsman, J. (no date) *Women, Violence, and Learning: What We Can Learn From Academic Writing.* Available at www.learningandviolence.net/helpothr/drawing.pdf, accessed on 29 April 2013.

Marcuse, H. (1964) *One Dimensional Man.* Boston, MA: Beacon Press.

Mojab, S. (ed.) (2010) *Women, War, Violence and Learning.* New York: Routledge.

O'Neill, E. and O'Sullivan, E.V. (2002) 'Transforming the Ecology of Violence: Ecology, War, Patriarchy, and the Institutionalization of Violence.' In E.V. O'Sullivan, A. Morrell and M.A. O'Connor (eds) *Expanding the Boundaries of Transformative Learning.* New York: Palgrave.

Republican Party of Texas (2012) *Report of the Platform Committee.* Austin: Republican Party of Texas. Available at www.texasgop.org/about-the-party, accessed on 29 April 2013.

Sandlin, J.A. (2007) 'Living and Learning in the Shadow of the Shopocalypse: Reverend Billy's Anti-Consumption Pedagogy-of-the-Unknown as Critical Adult Education.' In L. Servage and T. Fenwick (eds) *Proceedings of the 48th Adult Education Research Conference.* Halifax, Nova Scotia: Department of Adult Education, Mount Saint Vincent University.

Sinnott, J. (2009) 'Cognitive Development as the Dance of Adaptive Transformation.' In M.C. Smith and N. DeFrates-Densch (eds) *Handbook of Research on Adult Development.* New York: Routledge.

CHAPTER 13

STILL WATERS IN A STORM
THE POWER OF COLLECTIVE LEARNING

STEPHEN HAFF

All people are welcome at Still Waters, and we have all sorts of guests who come to visit. Some of them, I've learned, are pretty famous. What's cool is that none of us ever really know how famous they are. We just know that they come in, write with us and listen to our stories. I think that they understand that our stories are just as powerful as theirs. Still Waters has helped us feel that we can all write…(Analee, age 11)

I worked in mainstream education for over a decade. I was very committed to my work in a Brooklyn neighborhood called Bushwick, a beautiful and rough Hispanic ghetto, at the infamous Bushwick High School. It was a grand, old, six-storey, red-brick tower that looked like a prison or an antiquated mental hospital, where students would set hallway bulletin boards on fire and pose constant challenges to the teaching staff. Every day there were fights in the hallways and the lunch room and classrooms, brutal, bloody fights, heads slammed again and again on floors and chalk boards, hands turned to claws ripping at faces, all urged on by the screams of the delirious onlookers. I used to have to block the classroom doorway with my body to keep the kids from running into the hall to join a fight. I experienced a great deal of trauma in that school.

In addition to my classroom teaching, I ran a collective called Real People Theater, or RPT, a group of neighborhood teenagers who rewrote Shakespeare, Milton, and other classics, remixing the original text with Spanish and street slang. The success, by every measure, was astonishing. Kids who otherwise refused to read or write were choosing to master Shakespeare. We received huge acclaim in the press and among renowned theater artists. The *Village Voice* called us, "Nothing less than a revolution," and *The Brooklyn Rail* said we were, "One of the most respected theater collectives in New York City." Graciele Daniele, a revered Broadway director and choreographer, thanked us for, "bringing theater back to life." We were even adopted as the official apprentice company of the world-renowned Wooster Group. We traveled the globe. Kids who had been barely literate attended elite colleges.

In the end, working in that school was too much and I fell apart—the constant stress, challenge, and violence overwhelmed me and I needed to retreat and seek refuge with my parents back in Canada. Following three years of focused rehabilitation, surrounded by the same loving quiet that characterized my boyhood, I needed to go back to Brooklyn and make things right somehow. After several teaching jobs in rough neighborhoods, I finally left the system; I walked away, admitting that I could no longer struggle with students as a representative of values I didn't believe in. I felt a need to create a situation that was healthy for me and for students alike. So was born Still Waters in a Storm.

When I returned to Brooklyn I wanted to stay in touch with my students, those from before and after my breakdown, so I invited them to join me at a local pizzeria on Saturday afternoons, where we would eat and write together and listen to each other read out loud. There were no grades, no pressure, just an opportunity to be heard while sharing a meal. About a dozen young people, aged 14 to 25, showed up regularly. Then two children, a brother and sister aged six and eight whose father worked in the restaurant, became curious about what we were doing and joined in. Soon, more children followed them, and we had grown too big for the pizzeria. We needed a name. After a long discussion, we chose Still Waters in a Storm. As the kids explained, their lives were stormy, and this was a peaceful oasis, a refuge. Here, people were kind. They listened to each other's stories. We moved to our present classroom and continued to grow. Other parents saw children playing inside, reading, and writing, and asked if their children could join.

Word of mouth has spread and we now serve 30 families and have at least that many on our waiting list.

> When you open the door to school it's like a lifetime of jail. The windows are locked and the doors are guarded down. Spitballs are flying above you with spit hitting you. You see people picking on people, people screaming loud, no one paying attention to the teacher, throwing their stuff. This neighborhood is full of gangs that start fights. But here at Still Waters is calm and peaceful. Still Waters is a fun way to learn to read and write. It's not loud, and they help you a lot. When you can pay attention you can accomplish anything. I learned to read and write here when I was nine years old. Now I like reading a lot. The teachers here were pushing me and encouraging me to keep going. And the kids were the ones who said, "You can do it!" This place is like a home. I can write about my feelings. We are like a family. We listen to each other. We are nice to each other. (Solomon, age 10)

Still Waters has added Latin, Shakespeare, violin, homeschooling, and daily homework help to our offerings, and we have a stellar roster of guest writers who work with the group on Saturdays, including the Booker Prize-winning novelist Peter Carey, our chief adviser and advocate. All the services are free.

Through all the growing, our fundamental ritual remains the same. As many as 35 people gather, ages six and up, including children, teenagers, college students, and grown-ups. We eat pizza, and we write, about anything, in any style or genre, and any number of words. Then, we take turns reading our writings out loud and listening to each other. After each reading, the group responds, not by judging or correcting or liking or disliking, but by saying what we noticed, what we felt, what we related to, and by asking questions that encourage fullness and precision of expression. These responses say that we are listening with care.

> My experience at Still Waters is different because there's no uniform, you can wear make-up and there's no school on Fridays. And we start school at 12.30 and finish around 3.00. We are only nine kids and four adults, and we're not problem starters. There are no fights and no arguments. We start school talking about a topic, we laugh and then we start the

session and we bring up conversations and sometimes we say comments about our stories or writing or notes we took about the book we are reading. The teachers are nice. They help you when you need help. You could buy your food, we don't have to eat nasty school lunch. We are reading a great book called *A Tree Grows in Brooklyn*. I really like the book. We have school on the weekend. We get to play, have fun, and be nice to each other. We write and we read out loud and everybody listens, because we trust each other to talk about serious, personal stuff. We meet famous writers, we ask questions, and we get to play outside for a while. It's really fun. In the future when I grow up I want to be an artist and story writer. I love to write and draw. It's really awesome to become somebody new. (Lola, age 13)

The most important difference between Still Waters and my old classrooms, beside the obvious liberation from oppressive institutional practices such as streaming students best to worst, high-stakes testing, limited time, silence in the classroom, and students needing to ask permission to use the toilet or drink water, is that I am not doing the teaching alone anymore. I have learned to share the responsibility for giving attention by asking students to be attentive to each other. I guide the process, but I say, and do, less than ever before. The non-judgmental discussion reflects back to the writer the experience that the readers had. That information is far more valuable, both socially and academically and artistically, than spelling corrections or grades. With an authentic reason to write—namely, an audience who will ask for each other's reciprocal attention for no other reason than real interest and compassion— there is no need to threaten or to bribe anyone.

At Still Waters, our basic algorithm is this: everybody hears everybody.

That includes me. I am part of the group. I do wield executive power when needed to protect the algorithm. But apart from that, I write, I read aloud, I listen to people's responses to what I've written, I become vulnerable. This way, I not only model the activity I'm guiding, and share responsibility for the giving of attention, but I also receive attention.

A different life here at Still Waters: my life changed when I came to Still Waters because I finally found peace. I started getting better at math. Stephen Haff helped me a lot, for example:

he helped me in my math, my writing and my science. What is different between Still Waters and school is that Stephen and Doris don't hurry us up. They tell us the opposite. They tell us to take our time. They check our work, and they care about their work. My classmates here at Still Waters are real friends because we listen to each other, and because we can count on each other. One way I can count on my friends is to come pick me up from my house, and wait for me and walk with me to school. If the teacher assigns a project and one kid is late, another kid will help the late kid. We respect each other, because when I read my work out loud to them, they listen and leave everything they were doing to listen to me. And that makes me feel proud of me because I've found friends that are real friends. My writing has increased and improved because my friends respect me and listen to me. I love writing! (Penelope, age 11)

Back in the city school, a successful classroom "manager" (teachers in New York City are evaluated based on their "management" skills) could expect the attention of obedience. "Listen up" meant "Do as I say." In Still Waters, on the other hand, I feel listened to and cared for by the group, as a fellow human. Many, many times, students at Still Waters have asserted that the group is their "other family," and I feel the same way.

Schoolchildren are confined in abstraction for almost their entire childhood. Their personal, emotional lives have no place in school, where academic work is the focus. When are they supposed to reflect on who they are, and who they might become? When do they have the opportunity, the time, and the necessary conditions for deep study of themselves? A teenage girl at Still Waters wrote, "I love this quiet room. It reminds me who I am." But students in city schools are actively discouraged from writing or talking about anything too personal. If they write about their own feelings or experiences on the final high school English exams, they will fail. Interpersonal and intrapersonal intelligences are officially neglected. Even if the students don't know this consciously, their primal intuition knows, and they suffer.

My bad thing of old school: the things that are bad of my old school is that we are locked in for eight hours, eat lunch and play for 30 minutes, go home at 5.00. And a lot of pressure, a lot of mean kids, teachers are mean, they talk loud, you think they scream. They say you are bad at everything. And make you think you do no[t] know anything. They say you can not make it, but you can. They make you feel like if you had to leave school and be nothing. Still Waters: they let you eat. You can have a snack in the middle of the class. In Still Waters you are free, but you still study a lot, but less pressure. More reading, writing and science than in school. And I am more excited to come here, not scared. Not scared to do my writing and to spell bad. No mean kids, they are all nice. The teachers are soft, nice and good, and they listen. They talk nice, no screaming. They say you can do any career, like a chef or a doctor for dogs. And I love to write since I came to Still Waters. At my old school I will write just two pages because I would be scared to write what I want, and they would change what I wanted to express. I enjoy writing to people, and when they read it and when I read it out loud. We are connected. I have been writing about dogs, and people love the stories. Most of them have dogs. (Roxanne, age 8)

These are very old and obvious ideas, about neighborhood, family, and the proverbial village, but they can be important guides, even in an oppressive city school system that is charged with managing over a million children. Children find the imposition of structure by teachers and parents problematic and they're desperate to do things with a more flexible narrative. Perhaps this is counter-intuitive, but I believe that real freedom is achieved by taking real responsibility for our neighbors, that real freedom is a result of interdependence, of caring relationships—making the connections.

Such relationships can thrive even inside the Department of Education. I used to take my ninth graders down the street every week to work with first graders; they would read and write stories together, and answer each other's questions. Volatile teenagers who wanted to be home in bed and balked at mentoring small children were visibly happy when they saw the little ones waving at them and smiling, as they, the teenagers, awkwardly entered a room whose furniture they had long outgrown. The little ones helped the big ones belong somewhere, be needed by a real person, set them free from a life of abstraction, free from age segregation, free from a donkey's burden of textbooks, free from competition with their peers, free from measurement, free from lovelessness.

In school a student isn't allowed to be friends with the teacher. The teachers, some go just for money and don't really care how the students are learning. Some teachers have favorite students. As a little girl I was smart and the teacher never passed me and passed another girl. Teachers used to humiliate students in front of the whole class. In school I felt like a super dumb girl because I had low scores. Sometimes I fell asleep in class.

Because of Still Waters I love poetry and writing. We have freedom when it comes to using our imagination. He won't judge our writing and won't say it's incorrect. He pushes us and believes in us. He pushes where he knows we could get what we are capable of. (Nadia, age 13)

The word "love" can make educational practitioners uneasy. We're accustomed to curricula. I suppose "love" sounds fanciful, or unmanagerial. What does it mean, after all? But that very question can be a practical one. I keep asking, every day, how best to love the children in my care, knowing that they need to feel loved, and to learn how to love, as much as they need to read and write and do arithmetic; perhaps more. The novelist Richard Price described the atmosphere at Still Waters as one of "agenda-less empathy." I think that is a concise and accurate definition of love.

In a regular school it's almost like being in a jail. Schools have alarms and cameras like a jail. In school they tell you to do whatever they want you to do. You don't have choice. In school you have to beg the teacher to let you go to the bathroom. The reason why I got out of school was because I felt like I wasn't learning anything. After a while I hated school and didn't want to go anymore. But ever since I came to Still Waters I felt like part of me changed, not only my education but also me. I actually found myself. When I got into Still Waters I felt like I was free and my imagination traveled to different places I never imagined. When I came to this place I learned stuff that I never knew in my life.

Sometimes in my old school the teachers were in a bad mood. The students never listened, they were always noisy, and they didn't let you take notes with them fooling around in school. Still Waters is different from regular school. Stephen lets us got to the bathroom anytime we want. We explore with him. I feel like I learn everything with him. I actually do the stuff I like to do! In science I'm learning about dreams and how the brain works, something I always wanted to learn. I just never learned it in high school because I couldn't. I had to do whatever they told me to do. They picked out topics for us. Sometimes I didn't know if my opinion mattered to the teachers. They ignored me. I never used to raise my hand in high school because I thought they probably didn't even care. Still Waters is a new world for me, a new chapter in my life. Whenever I feel down, my Still Waters group comes and asks me what happens to me. I feel like this is my second family. I care about each person in here. I feel welcomed here. When you feel better you learn better. In Still Waters I get to write stuff that I never knew I would say. I write my personal writing and read it out loud, because I feel trust and thanking everyone for listening to me. (Magdalena, age 14)

The Still Waters ritual of writing, reading, listening, and responding is practice in love. When the time comes to listen to each other read our writing out loud, I remind the group, always, that one of the greatest gifts we can give anyone else is listening—really listening—and when we are really listening we compose our bodies, in the same way as writers, we compose our thoughts and write them on paper. I remind them that we are called "Still Waters," not "Squirmy Waters," and that this stillness is not the immobility of obedience, but an offering of peace and mutual respect. It is a loving stillness, just as the silence that accompanies a reading is not the paralyzed voice of students in fear, but a deep and sacred hush, a loving quiet, the same loving quiet that brought me back from depression.

Within the context of Still Waters we still need guidelines and a loose structure.

1. You are both a guide and a member of the group. You model full participation and vulnerability: writing, reciting, listening, and responding.

2. You facilitate discussion by acknowledging those who want to speak and gently but firmly insisting on, "one voice at a time."

3. You protect the group from outside interference or inside sabotage during the session. Make the boundaries, and their rationale, firm and consistent. You're all here to put thoughts and feelings into words, and to reflect back to each other what you've heard.

4. You remind members, as necessary, that they are to respond by noticing details, asking questions, and making connections, never by judging what they hear or telling anyone what to write.

5. You remind members, as necessary, that they are to refrain from praising each other, announcing likes or dislikes. Praise can become the goal and interfere with the writing process.

6. You never correct writing or speaking, but gradually introduce possible ways for writers to make their self-expression more precise or visible (metaphors, alternate vocabulary).

7. You learn by truly caring about what the students say, by listening with compassion and patience. Writing that seems like nonsense or offense is probably beginning to say something that may not completely emerge until much later in the process.

8. This is also the example you set for the group: listening with compassion and patience.

9. You learn by accepting with gratitude what the group says in response to your own writing.

10. You learn by reaching always for fullness and clarity of expression in your writing and speaking. You admit to confusion and frustration in your own writing and thinking, as a natural part of the process. You follow a student's example and acknowledge that you are doing so. Your humility and effort will demystify the process for the group.

11. There is no agenda except self-expression and compassion. No final project, no test, no homework. This is sacred time.

12. There is no vision for how the people in the group should be as a result of this. Only the freedom to express themselves and the responsibility to listen with compassion during this time. The rest is up to them.

CHAPTER 14

RESISTING THE CHARM OF AN ALL-CONSUMING LIFE?

RIOTS, REBELLION AND FINDING NEW UTOPIAS FOR CHILDREN AND YOUNG PEOPLE

DR ADAM BARNARD

This chapter offers some directions for resistance to 'consumption' for children and young people. It starts with the 'promise of neo-liberalism' as the current economic situation that gives a 'gilt-edged' promise and the construction of 'consuming children' and young people. Having established the type of society that this generation of children inherits, the discussion moves to consider the tradition of utopian thought that provides alternative, competing and different visions of the possibilities of childhood and youth. The 'impulse' or structure of feeling presents a challenge to the construction of the dominant idea of 'consuming children'. The final part of the chapter suggests some escape routes or exit strategies from consumption through resistance.

WHERE ARE WE NOW?

The commercialisation of childhood gives rise to emotional distress, a rise in 'mental health' issues for the next generation and the neo-liberal market agenda redefining childhood. These changes are constructing 'children as consumers' as a major feature of the current landscape. Children, childhood and young people have been pushed by neo-liberalism to become objectified targets for advertising, thought of as market opportunities, commodities and consumers.

Neo-liberalism is now part of the current stage of 'selfish capitalism', as introduced by Oliver James in the Foreword. 'Selfish capitalism strongly promotes materialistic values and their behavioural manifestation – compulsive consumerism' (James 2009, p.165). James (2009) suggests emotional distress for children and young people is more developed in capitalist societies, and sees this form of materialism as leading to greater distress, emotional insecurity, poor personal relationships, inauthenticity, a lack of autonomy and lower self-esteem amongst children and young people. The British market for children's consumer goods is now worth £30 billion and the commercialisation of childhood is well-established (James 2009). Children and young people are the targets of an increasingly aggressive form of marketing. For example, Nairn (2008, p.239), reviewing strategies and ways to target young consumers, suggests:

> a great deal of advertising is poorly labelled and deceptively integrated into content. Most sites visited by children are created for an adult audience which means 25 percent of adverts were for dating, gambling, loans, surgery and age-restricted products. There was also evidence of pester power, dubious 'free' offers and incitement to make impulse purchases using mobile phone credit.

Selfish capitalism and its support by materialism changes children and young people into consumers and creates an impoverished lifestyle.

So where would the challenge against the unfulfilled promise of consumer society offering a vacant materialism and emerge to a valuing of childhood for children and youth? Perhaps strategies and ways to resist consumerism and materialism offer us some hope. Given the situation, is there a need to protect children from corporate marketing under neo-liberal, 'selfish' capitalism?

UTOPIA

The tradition of utopian thought provides a rich and alternative narrative or story of commercialisation. Claeys and Tower Sargent (1999) provide a helpful guide to the tradition of utopianism and produce a telling portrait of civilisation's need to imagine and construct ideal societies. They suggest, 'Utopianism generally is the imaginative project, positive of negative, of a society that is substantially different from the one in which the author lives' (Claeys and Tower Sargent 1999, p.1). They also suggest (1999) four main historical stages in the evolution of utopian traditions. First, religious radicalism in the sixteenth and seventeenth century laid by egalitarian schemes of communal property holding resulting in utopian socialism in the nineteenth century. Second, voyages of discovery concerning virtues and vices and the corrupting influence of increasing wealth threatening moral degeneration. Third, scientific discovery and technological innovation held the promise of indefinite progress and hopes and fears of future developments. Finally, aspirations for greater social equality emerged in the revolutionary movements of the later eighteenth century. These traditions represent alternative ways of expressing the utopian impulse, and utopia has a form, function and purpose (Levitas 1990) as an alternative way of living or an alternative sensibility or responsiveness to the prevailing or usual ideas.

So where might we find the utopia impulse that surfaces in covert ways for and against commercialisation and consumption?

The utopia of no-place emerged through the twentieth century as 'home', as the Wizard of Oz suggests, 'there's no place like home'. The 'home' offered the possibility of care, concern, sanctuary and nourishment. Away from the alienated world of work, from the dangers of public life, and the threat of the outside, the home became the utopian imaginary of a better place. The twentieth century has seen the 'home' colonised not for care and concern but as the site for consumption. The 'home' became the marketplace and site for consuming the post-war proliferation of domestic consumables. Children and young people became the essential bridge for domestic consumption. 'Children have become the conduits from the consumer market place into the household, the link between advertisers and the family purse' (Schor 2004, p.11). The age of conspicuous consumption and consumer lifestyles (Featherstone 1987) has drawn families into this consumer lifestyle.

However, there are cracks in the mirror of the false promise of commercialism, the glimpse of other ways of living and the possibilities of another place to a rich, human and fulfilled utopia.

THE MCDONALDISATION OF CHILDHOOD

George Ritzer (1995, p.2010) has applied the German sociologist Max Weber's understanding of rationalisation as the dominant form of related processes by which every aspect of human action became subject to calculation, measurement and control. The concept of rationalisation was thus part of Weber's view of capitalist society as an 'iron cage' in which the individual, stripped of religious meaning (disenchantment) and moral value, would be increasingly subject to government surveillance and bureaucratic regulation. This surveillance and regulation is through efficiency, prediction, control and the replacement of human labour with non-human technology. Ritzer (1995, 2010) suggests this is a contemporary form of McDonaldisation.

The first dimension of McDonaldisation, efficiency is the search for ever-greater efficiency, can take many different forms, but in 'McDonaldizing systems, it has taken the form primarily of streamlining a variety of processes, simplifying goods and services, and using the customer to perform work that paid employees used to do' (Ritzer 1995, p.58). Calculability, the second dimension of McDonaldisation, involves an emphasis on quantity rather than quality. This emphasis shows up, 'in various ways, but especially in the focus on quantity rather than quality of products, the widespread efforts to create the illusion of quantity, and the tendency to reduce production and service processes to numbers' (Ritzer 1995, p.78). Predictability is the third dimension of McDonaldisation that:

> involves the emphasis on things such as discipline, systematization, and routine so that things are the same from one time or place to another. Predictability is achieved in various ways, including the replication of settings, the use of scripts to control what employees say, the routinization of employee behaviour, and the offering of uniform products. (Ritzer 1995, p.99)

The fourth dimension of McDonaldization is the replacement of human with nonhuman technology. The most important element of this is control over the uncertainties created by employees. In controlling employees, nonhuman technologies also lead to greater control over work-related processes as well as the finished product. The ultimate in control is reached when employees are replaced by nonhuman technologies such as robots. Nonhuman technologies are also employed to control the uncertainties created by customers. The objective is to make them more pliant participants in McDonaldized processes. (Ritzer 1995, p.120)

From Ritzer's generalist applications of understanding the growth of control over many social activities, parenting, childrearing and child protection have also been subject to McDonaldisation.

An example of the McDonaldisation of children and young people can be found in thoughtful critiques of child protection systems. For example, Ferguson's (1997) perspective is based entirely on a critique of the bureaucratic, instrumentally rational features of modern child protection systems. With its sole emphasis on constraint and control, it constitutes a one-dimensional, monolithic view of developments in child welfare and social work. Child protection is driven by the same imperatives of McDonaldisation.

Giroux (2009) presents an analysis of contemporary society in the way neo-liberalism has marginalised and treated youth as disposable objects. 'In a radical free-market culture, [or neo-liberal] when hope is precarious and bound to commodities and a corrupt financial system, young people are no longer at risk: they are the risk' (Giroux 2009, p.x). For Giroux, media representations of youth and young people confirm or support state interventions and policies. Youth and young people have been demonised as, 'variously lazy, stupid, self-indulgent, volatile, dangerous, and manipulative' (Giroux 2009, p.14). The repressive state apparatus's response to the summer of riots in the UK in 2011 has reinforced this vision and understanding of youth, creating a climate of fear, distrust and disinterest in the next generation. We no longer fear for our children, their fate, safety, inheritance and well-being; we fear them. Giroux (2009) charts the form of governing under neo-liberalism as it creates youth to consume. It 'locks up' youth with aggressive criminal and penal policy and 'locks them out' from academic freedom in education, before casting youth 'into a shadow in the gilded age' as the 'age of disposability'. The disposability of youth is the new emerging form of relations creating the possibility of 'significant harm' to the next generation.

The rise of neo-liberalism and the dominance of markets with the cutting of state provision has ended the social contract or obligation of adult society to future generations. This relationship has become characteristic of contemporary society for youth. When the young do not consume, they are criminalised or pushed into entrepreneurial schooling with the erosion of services supporting youth, conceived as objects, and have the possibility of challenge or action removed (Giroux 2009, p.23). The experience of marginalised, criminalised and exploited youth has led to urban outcasts (Wacquant 2007) or youth as 'collateral damage' (Bauman 2011). The current system of 'embedded liberalism' is usually used to, 'signal how market processes and entrepreneurial and corporate activities' are 'surrounded by a web of social and political constraints and a regulatory environment that sometimes restrained but in other instances led the way in economic and industrial strategy' for identifying neoliberalism as the new orthodoxy (Harvey 2005, p.11). With the dominance of these ideas and ways of working, children and young people's horizons have been limited and their possibilities closed down.

This new orthodoxy is reflected in state policies and the experiences in everyday life. Donzelot (1979) provides a historical study of the family not just as a history of everyday life but in the family's use as an object of social policy and intervention. Using case studies he analyses how the family is moulded by state intervention to fulfil specific functions. Once families are seen to fail in their assigned roles, this acts as a trigger for ever-more sophisticated and systematic forms of state intervention. For example, early intervention and early help are the new watchwords of services provided by local authorities.

Donzelot (1979) charts the shift of 'protected liberation', freeing children from vulgar fears and constraints such as in the Victorian family, to 'supervised freedom' in the school and employing techniques to shepherd children into spaces that could be closely watched. He suggests 'what was at issue, then, was the transition from a government of families to a government through the family' (Donzelot 1979, p.92). This control of state intervention further worsens the repressive and oppressed situation of youth and children. The family as a state instrument of control embeds consumption into all activities of the private sphere.

For example, 'having a room of one's own' is a desire of many children but it also becomes a means of control. 'Go to your room,' for a harassed parent, becomes a way of interrupting disruptive behaviour and consigning the child to an absent space from the family. Once in that space the child finds solace in those material objects within their own bedroom. The thorough saturation of commercial commodities becomes the salve and comfort for difficult family relationships.

The fusion of families and commodities has created a neo-liberal orthodoxy. Against this orthodoxy, Ferguson (1997) shows how, as knowledgeable human actors, people actively make themselves the subjects with the ability to act and not just the objects (passive objects) of social processes (Beck, Giddens and Lash 1994; Berman 1983; Frisby 1985). Actively making ourselves in the ways we see fit can work against neo-liberalism, but how can this happen?

RESISTANCE

In such a situation, how can children and young people resist these processes? A utopian impulse with a political programme can inform future developments. The promise of utopia is an unrealised potential that can challenge the consumption-driven household, the McDonaldised of children and young people, and bureaucratic instrumental responses to child protection.

The changing infrastructure and neo-liberalism has opened new spaces for children and young people to resist capitalism, neo-liberalism and consumption (Christensen, Jansson and Christensen 2010). It has also provoked community-based activity, away from state regulation, such as 'Reclaim the Streets' to make roads play spaces for children and young people. A 'Do-It-Yourself' ethos has developed to open spaces for convivial relations and activities, against regulation, state supervision and control. This ethos, sensibility and structure of feeling has problematised understandings of childhood (Rothschild 2005) and the state's response to children and young people (Fox Harding 1997), and lends itself to the utopian impulse for resistive politics or a happy future filled with promise.

The development of a politics of resistance would challenge the repressive features of culture while developing a local and global politics predicated on new ways of expression, representation and protest in the name of human features and dignity (Guattari and Negri 1990). For example, the politics of resistance is expressed well in alternative forms of contemporary culture.

Ben Drew, a British rapper, singer-songwriter, actor and film director who performs under the name Plan B, echoes the resistance and challenge presented to society through his work. His lyrics are inspired by growing up in the environment of inner-city, economically marginalised and socially excluded London. The first song in Ill Manors, itself called 'Ill Manors', is a protest song concerning the 2011 London riots. It satirises the presentation of disadvantaged British urban youth. Plan B regularly questions the image of British youth represented in the media, criticising the class system, social exclusion and the lack of social justice. He condemns David Cameron's Conservative Party as trapping the poor in their situation. The social divisions and exclusions are papered over in a veneer of achievement and representations of an inclusive Britain.

Plan B talks of a 'folk deviling' of young men and women from deprived areas, and the derogatory association with the word 'chav'. For him, this word is akin to a racist or homophobic slur, but the media and the public at large use it to categorise these young men and women often and openly. Depicted in the media as benefit claimants, unemployed and petty criminals, this term only marginalises these young people more. Plan B seeks to highlight deprivation and disadvantage as issues that led to the UK riots in 2011. They are not inborn, and are not characteristics specific to a person. They stem from state indifference to the social and economic inequalities that exist in different areas, especially in a society such as the UK that champions consumerism over its people.

It is from this backdrop that the promise of utopia beckons. There are well-trodden routes to this promise in the face of consumer capitalism. For example, the leader of Situationist International (SI), Guy Debord, provides an alternative story.

Debord's exhortation for the 'revolution of everyday life' was for an overarching desire for a rich life, full of passion not passive contemplation. For Debord, contemporary society is based on commodity production and the notion of the spectacle, which provides a utility in the construction of a critical theory of contemporary society (Jappe 1999, p.3). The economy has brought human life under the sway of its own laws rather than being economically driven.

Debord's understanding of the society of the spectacle, in the first instance, is the downgrading of 'being' into 'having'. The rise of capitalism has emptied everyday life of meaning, fullness and activity, to possession, commodities and production. With the rise of consumer capitalism 'having' has been further downgraded to 'appearing' (Debord 1995, Thesis 17). Jappe (1999, p.5) suggests:

> Debord's analysis is based on the everyday experience of the impoverishment of life, its fragmentation into more and more widely separated spheres, and the disappearance of any unitary aspects at the level of the image. Everything life lacks is to be found in the spectacle, conceived as an ensemble of independent representations.

For example, the rise of vapid cultural celebrity, the need to be famous not for a lasting corpus of quality work but to just be seen as famous, and isolated individuals 'lost' in the stream of spectacular relations. The temporality of consumption has commodified time with workers being subjected to, 'the violent appropriation of their time' (Debord 1995, p.159). The leisure time of the weekend is co-opted and commodified, set aside for consumption.

Debord's solution is the conviction that the whole world must be torn down then rebuilt, not under the sign of the economy but instead under that of generalised creativity (Jappe 1999, p.47). The situations that are advocated were the 'complete and authentic construction of situations', which meant a, 'new urbanism in which all the arts would be mobilised in the creation of a passion-filled atmosphere' (Jappe 1999, p.59) in the creation of situations and the 'civilisation of play'. A playful future rather than one to buy is the alternative story to neo-liberalism.

MANIFESTO FOR RESISTANCE

From the situation of 'consuming children', to the promise of utopia, the McDonaldisation of childhood, the disposability of youth and government through the family in the age of disposability, creativity, creating situations and a 'civilisation of play' offer a vision of the utopian impulse and political project to reject neo-liberal consumerism.

Where might we find examples of the practice of utopian principles and resistance? We can have a broad hostility to the consumerism and materialism of the contemporary era, but where do we find the cracks in the mirror of neo-liberalism capitalism? Agitators, activists and artists contribute to the alternative histories, stories and representations with the promise of utopia.

hooks (1994) examines the interplay of popular culture and voices of diaspora (of dispersed populations) as a powerful site for intervention, challenge and change. It is in the genre of popular culture that production, consumption and cultural politics can be critically developed. This politics of difference (West 1992) is unified by the challenge to the existing structure of ideas and actions (youth as outcasts or outlaws), the myths that are made (such as disruptive youth) and encouraging activism for the development of new forms of culture for distributive justice, social inclusion and empowerment. Youth, ethnicity and gender are commodified as an object and able to be consumed by various audiences. Against this process is the possibility to reclaim the mental environment from the influence of multinationals and the corporate state's mission to keep capitalism expanding. Understanding the roots of domination clarifies the routes we must take to resist, and critical thinking is the gift to realise the passage to utopia as we become enlightened witnesses.

Routes of resistance show encouraging signs of emerging when young people make their own protest and raise their own voices to articulate their concerns. Plan B's contribution to resistance is the 'true, dark reality' of youths' contemporary experience. 'Ill Manors' is seen as the greatest British protest song in years.

Klein (2000) offers one direction for a strategic movement against the spectacle with her *No Logo* and 'culture jamming', which emerged in the mid-1980s. She argues that it, 'was Guy Debord and the Situationists...who first articulated the power of a simple détournement, defined as an image, message or artefact lifted out of its context to create and give new meaning' (Klein 2001, p.282).

She goes on:

for years, we in this movement have fed off our opponent's symbols – their brands, their office towers, their photo opportunity summits. We have used them as rallying cries, as focal points, as popular education tools. But these symbols were never the real targets; they were the levers, the handles. The symbols were only ever doorways. It's time to walk through them. (Klein 2001, p.32)

Culture-jamming and 'adbusting' is the strategic response identified by Klein (2000) that parallels the Situationists' response to the spectacle, and embodies the contemporary forms of détournement that are the positive legacy of SI. Culture-jammers hacking into corporate advertising and corporate speech make 'pointedly political' messages. These alternative messages are Situationist tools, 'used, loaned and borrowed and in a much broader political movement against branded life' (Klein 2000, p.309). The power of the visual and using the images of spectacle turned back on itself to illuminate the contradictory, damaging and exploitative relations. *Meme War*, by Adbusters editor Kalle Lasn, uses startling images to make challenging political points and observations such as the drug-snorting of people, the assassination of capitalism, the romance of 'darling, let's go deeply into debt', 'fight the nothingness', the bowels of capitalism and the organised crime of brand bullies. The 'economy needs you to keep consuming' as a salve for the sickness of modern economics, as the discipline of economics has become a mathematical game without practical relevance or consequences (Lasn 2012).

'The demand…is to build a resistance – both high-tech and grassroots, both focused and fragmented – that is as global, and as capable of coordinated action, as the multinationals it seeks to subvert' (Klein 2000, p.446). All forms of social life – schooling, education, entertainment, leisure, politics and everyday life – are increasingly spectacularised: banal, passive and unfulfilling. The advent of new technologies – the internet, video games and multi-media – will do nothing to abate the relentless march of the spectacle.

Graffiti artists, anti-globalisation protestors, guerrilla gardeners, allotment owners, co-operatives, community projects, small-scale producers and independent creators all embody a creative impulse that is not mediated by the spectacle. They aim at forms of creative and artistic expression on a human scale, to challenge dominant forms of consumption and to produce cultural, artistic and political forms of resistance. For children and young people, an alternative to corporate capitalism's vacuous promises needs to be made through alternative thinking, feeling and action of creative play.

MODEST MAKERS

A maker is a person who fashions, constructs, prepares for use, or manufactures something – a manufacturer. Resistance to the pre-packaged world of consumerism presents opportunities of a new generation of makers who creatively construct a more convivial, sensitive and alternatively purposed world. Children and young people are producers and makers, not consuming spectators. The legacy of making an alternative world is the one the next generation should inherit, not a pre-packaged world of consumption. To make differently, we need to think differently.

Children's worlds are increasing prescribed and co-opted by the dominant narratives of consumer capitalism. What is required is an alternative story on the fullness of being a child, on the richness of human potential, an alternative (re)storying on the wonderment of creative living for the art of change. We need to re-store and restory a full, human life, grounded in the everyday, infused with art, creativity and making infused with a utopian impulse. Feeling and acting also require thinking. 'Good thinking' is the conclusion that Munro (2008) arrives at for effective child protection. Good thinking, under the principle of the utopian impulse, is to think differently.

Thinking differently provides an alternative view of the world, a creative restorying that is perspectival (by challenging and changing the perspective through which we view the world), prospective (seeing things not immediately present, as a forward-looking representational landscape), and perceptive (having or showing insight, discerning, intelligent). The utopian impulse is infused with meaning along these guiding principles. The utopian project as a political programme for change follows the doctrine of the three Rs – refinement, reduction, replacement (Woolf 2011, p.204) but we might add recycle, repair, reinvigorate, repurpose. A cluster of utopian principles informs a utopian practice and an ethical sensibility that resists the imperatives of McDonalds and neo-liberal consumption. For a lived experience of the everyday fused with meaning and significance, and ethos and sensibility of justice, it is necessary for a critique of capitalism for its disastrous effects on the population in general and children and young people in particular. A reconnection with alternative values, ethics and ethos to promote human dignity and social justice alongside different forms of representation presents different possibilities for radically different identities, formations, creations and expressions for children and young people to explore and enjoy.

CONCLUSION

The road to change is not easy and demands a level of engagement and understanding. This chapter has reviewed the type of society that the new generation of children and young people are to inherit. The promise of neo-liberalism has promoted a selfish capitalism with its disastrous consequences for children and young people. The utopian tradition offers an alternative to this form of capitalism. The McDonaldisation of childhood is the contemporary drive to rationalise problematic youth and has triggered more oppressive and authoritarian controls such as a generation of disposable youth with highly repressive, supervised freedom. Resistance to these forces are manifest in numerous and conflicting ways. Signposts for these possibilities exist with alternative storying, alternative making, creativity and thinking differently. Children and young people have a future to make in their own image.

REFERENCES

Bauman, Z. (2011) *Collateral Damage: Social Inequalities in a Global Age*. London: Wiley & Sons.

Beck, U., Giddens, A. and Lasch, S. (1994) *Reflexive Modernization*. Cambridge: Polity Press.

Berman, M. (1983) *All That Is Solid Melts into Air: The Experience of Modernity*. London: Verso.

Christensen, M., Jansson, A. and Christensen, C. (2010) *Online Territories: Globalization, Mediated Practice, and Social Space*. New York: Peter Lang.

Claeys, G. and Tower Sargent, L. (1999) *The Utopian Reader*. London: New York University Press.

Debord, G. (1995) *The Society of the Spectacle*. (Translation by D. Nicholson-Smith.) New York: Zone Books.

Donzelot, J. (1979) *The Policing of Families*. (Translation by R. Hurley.) London: Hutchinson & Co.

Featherstone, M. (1987) 'Lifestyle and consumer culture.' *Theory, Culture and Society, 1*, 18–33.

Ferguson, H. (1997) 'Protecting children in new times: child protection and the risk society.' *Child and Family Social Work, 2*, 4, 221–234.

Fox Harding L. (1997) *Perspectives in Childcare Policy*. London: Longman.

Frisby, D. (1985) *Fragments of Modernity*. Cambridge: Polity Press.

Giroux, H. (2009) *Theory and Resistance in Education: Towards a Pedagogy for the Opposition*. Westport, CT: Greenwood Publishing.

Guattari, F. and Negri, A. (1990) *Communist Like Us*. Paris: Semiotext.

Harvey, D. (2005) *A Brief History of Neo-Liberalism*. Oxford: Oxford University Press.

hooks, b. (1994) *Outlaw Culture: Resisting Representation*. London: Routledge.

James, O. (2009) *Selfish Capitalism*. London: Verso.

Jappe, A. (1999) *Guy Debord*. (Translation by D. Nicholson-Smith.) Berkeley, CA: University of California Press.

Klein, N. (2000) *No Logo: Taking Aim at the Brand Bullies*. London: Flamingo.

Klein, N. (2001) 'Between McWorld and Jihad.' *The Guardian Weekend*, 27 October, 30–33.

Lasn, K. (2012) *Meme Wars*. London: Penguin.

Levitas, R. (1990) *The Concept of Utopia*. London: Philip Allen.

Munro, E. (2008) *Effective Child Protection* (2nd edition). London: Sage Publications.

Nairn, A. (2008) '"It does my head in … buy it, buy it, buy it!" The commercialisation of UK children's web sites.' *Young Consumers: Insight and Ideas for Responsible Marketers, 9*, 4, 239–253.

Ritzer, G. (1995) *The McDonaldizisation of Society: An Investigation into the Changing Character of Contemporary Social Life*. London: Pine Forge.

Ritzer, G. (2010) *McDonaldizisation: The Reader*. Thousand Oaks, CA: Pine Forge Press.

Rothschild, J. (2005) *The Dream of the Perfect Child*. Bloomington, IN: Indiana University Press.

Schor, J. (2004) *Born to Buy: The Commercialized Child and the New Consumer Culture*. New York: Scribner.

Wacquant, L. (2007) *Urban Outcasts: A Comparative Sociology of Advanced Marginality*. London: Polity Press.

West, C. (1992) 'The Postmodern Crisis of the Black Intellectuals.' In L. Grossberg, C. Nelson and P. Treichely (eds) *Cultural Studies*. London: Routledge.

Woolf, J. (2011) *Ethics and Public Policy: A Philosophical Inquiry*. London: Routledge.

CHAPTER 15

CONCLUSION

A NEW CATEGORY OF CHILD ABUSE?

JIM WILD

...and contemporary psychology, sociology and economic science are all complicit in the fiasco. So the time has come to deconstruct all the assumptive notions involved – object, need, aspiration, consumption itself...and it is the working processes of an unconscious social logic that must be retrieved beneath the consecrated ideology of consumption.

(Jean Baudrillard, *The Consumption Reader*, p.255)

The consequence of this corporate capture of childhood is not only being felt by children, who are becoming more materialistic, overweight, stressed, depressed and self-destructive. Advertising and marketing aim to make these future citizens dissatisfied with what they have and want to consume more. Yet the health of the planet requires us to consume less. What is more, by undermining the critical thinking faculties of future generations corporations are depriving them of the ability to solve pressing social and environmental problems; problems such as global warming, species extinction and water shortages, which are in many ways caused or exacerbated by those very corporations that are attempting to breed subservient employees and dumbed-down citizens. (Beder, Varney and Gosden 2009, p.223)

This book has attempted to pull together a diverse range of concerns about how commercial, corporate and sexual exploitation have negative and harmful effects on children and young people. Its primary intention has been to pose a controversial question: has commercial, corporate and sexual exploitation reached such undesirable and crazed levels that children and young people are now 'significantly harmed' by the effects? It is a serious question, one that requires critical thinking and clarity of judgement in our reflections about the sort of society we want and the values we wish to uphold.

In the introduction I featured some adapted key questions for social workers when considering harm being caused to children, which I outline again below:

- What is the nature of the commercial or corporate targeting and in what context are we exploring these concerns?

- Is there an impact on the child's health and development and is there any objective evidence that corporate and commercial targeting have adverse effects on children and young people?

- What is its significance – the extent of the impact on the child or young person in the short, medium and long term?

- What are the psychological effects – on well-being, self-esteem and identity?

- What is the level of targeting – its extent, duration and frequency?

- What ability do children and young people have to give objective consent and informed knowledge when they are targeted?

When considered alongside the contributions made in each chapter, it's clear that these issues do pose difficult questions to those involved in child welfare and child protection today.

Inevitably the conclusions drawn by me, by the contributors of this book and by you the reader will be subjective. We still have yet to see the level of research and scientific study needed to fully quantify the impact of this harm, and our response is inevitably informed by our politics: our views on how the world should be shaped and governed, and our own sense of what is legitimate and acceptable in a consumer society.

Perhaps the most obvious area we can *see* the evidence is that of junk food. It is reasonable to expect that further down the line there will be some sort of government intervention simply on the basis of the demands placed on the health service from obese young people who will emerge into early adulthood with specific health problems and life-threatening diseases – and yet those concerned with child welfare and child protection should surely have seen these as emerging issues decades ago? Are we not complicit in this terrible manipulation of the minds of young people to the point they are unable to distinguish between healthy food and items that are, in reality, poison? Are successive governments so 'in the pockets' of multi-national food producers they fear the consequences of passing robust legislation that could save lives? These questions are real dilemmas and can give rise to feelings of powerlessness on the part of those with responsibility for protecting children.

In a world where billions are spent to target children and young people we should ask the following questions:

- How can professionals who work with children and young people and parents take effective action to counter these issues?

- Do Local Safeguarding Children Boards simply ignore the wider definitions of significant harm and challenges in this publication and not debate the issues?

- At a local level how can we draw attention to these issues?

- With globalisation so fixed in our economies are those *we* elect to govern us unwilling to take action?

- What can we do within our own private and professional lives – whether child protection specialists, schools, communities or families?

Many of the problems we are considering now were identified by others decades ago.

Marcuse is the author of a now classic publication *One Dimensional Man*, which was published in 1964 and offers a critique of contemporary capitalism and communist society, identifying a parallel rise in social repression. At the beginning of the book he states that: 'The people recognize themselves in their commodities; they find their soul in their automobile, hi-fi set, split-level home, kitchen equipment...'

Eric Fromm also raised critical issues about the sort of society we are manufacturing in a range of publications from the late 1950s onwards. In his final publication of 1976, *To Have or To Be?*, Fromm explores the hazards of materialism: 'The overall effect of advertising is to stimulate the craving for consumption…'

Each decade has given us great thinkers who have warned about the perils of globalisation and a sense of dismay with the values associated with consumerism, as well as more recently the more dubious benefits of the internet. These individuals have for the most part been ignored in preference of a version of society based on one single overriding preoccupation – consumption.

One author, the late Neil Postman in his book *The Disappearance of Childhood* (1982), suggested that parents can make a difference:

Specifically, resistance entails conceiving of parenting as an act of rebellion against American culture…but most rebellious of all is to attempt to control the media's access to one's children… the first way is to limit the amount of exposure children have to media. The second is to monitor carefully what they are exposed to, and to provide them with a continuously running critique of the themes and values of the media's content…(p.153)

Whilst written in 1982, when Postman could not conceive the range of new technologies likely to emerge over the forthcoming decades, I think his advice still rings true in some respects whilst always against a backdrop of overwhelming forces at work to subvert the most dedicated parent.

We need to understand that these issues permeate the lives of children and young people – not as episodic or isolated events but in forms that are relentless, all-consuming and overwhelming, as described in the chapters within this book. Their minds are subject to constant creative and insidious forms of marketing from companies and corporations, which many of us outside the worlds of advertising and marketing would see as a waste of creativity and talent: inappropriately conceived, without a moral compass and with little or no idea of the long-term effects or consequences of their actions.

It is my expectation that the problems highlighted in this book will resurface again and again as they become increasingly of concern and in need of statutory intervention or state regulation.

This book raises questions in relation to child welfare, but in doing so inevitably also poses wider questions relating to the legitimacy of unregulated neo-liberalism and its relationship to society's values.

In children's services there has always been a widely held view that early intervention can result in more positive outcomes for children and young people; perhaps this publication is a little late in this respect, but it is the first to suggest we are abusing and maltreating children and young people through these practices, and I hope it will act as a catalyst for reflection and a call to those charged with the protection and welfare of children and young people to take action.

REFERENCES

Beder, S., Varney, W. and Gosden, R. (2009) *This Little Kiddy Went To Market: The Corporate Capture of Childhood.* London: Pluto Press.

Clarke, D.B., Coel, M.A. and Housiaux, K.M.L. (eds) (2003) *The Consumption Reader.* London: Routledge.

Fromm, E. (1976) *To Have or To Be?* New York: Harper and Row.

Marcuse, H. (1964) *One Dimensional Man.* Boston, MA: Beacon Press.

Postman, N. (1982) *The Disappearance of Childhood.* New York: Delacorte Press.

LIST OF CONTRIBUTORS

Jim Wild is the lead trainer and founder of The Centre for Active and Ethical Learning and editor of this publication. Jim has spent over three decades in child protection as a frontline worker, manager and trainer. He is editor of several publications including *Working with Men for Change* (Routledge, 1998), *The Value-base of Social Work and Social Care* (Open University Press, 2008) and *Fit for Practice in Child Protection* (Reconstruct Training, 2004). Jim spent two years planning three events that have led to this publication. Some keynotes from the events are available to view at www.activelearningcpac.org.uk

Oliver James obtained his degree in Social Anthropology at the University of Cambridge, UK, and trained as a child clinical psychologist at the University of Nottingham, UK. He worked as a research fellow at Brunel University, London, before occupying an NHS post as a clinical psychologist for six years at the Cassel Hospital in London. He became a journalist, bestselling author and television documentary producer and presenter. He is a prolific writer and his latest publications include *Love Bombing: Reset Your Child's Emotional Thermostat* (Karnac Books, 2012) and *Office Politics* (Vermilion, 2013).

Professor Agnes Nairn is a leading researcher, writer, consultant and speaker on the impact of marketing on children. In addition to award-winning academic papers, she co-authored the book *Consumer Kids* (Constable, 2009), the UNICEF report *Children's Wellbeing in the UK, Spain and Sweden* and the Family and Parenting report *Advergames: It's Not Child's Play*. She advises government on regulatory policy and is a frequent media commentator on the ethics of marketing to children; see www.agnesnairn.co.uk.

Tim Lobstein has campaigned on food issues since the 1970s, helping author *Food and Profit: It Makes you Sick* followed by books in the 1980s (*Fast Food Facts*, Camden Press, 1988 and *Children's Food: The Good, the Bad and the Ugly*) and subsequent work with the UK Food Commission and the World Health Organization promoting stronger controls on marketing food to children. He is now Adjunct Professor of Public Health Advocacy at Curtin University, Western Australia, and Policy Director at the International Obesity Task Force.

Dr Wayne Warburton is a psychologist, Lecturer in Developmental Psychology with the Department of Psychology at Macquarie University (Sydney), and Deputy Director of the Children and Families Research Centre. Wayne's research and publications primarily examine aggressive behaviour, with a strong focus on the effects of violent media. Wayne's most recent book, *Growing Up Fast and Furious* (with Danya Braunstein, The Federation Press, 2012) describes the latest scientific findings in plain language, and has been acclaimed by scholars, professionals and parents alike.

James Hawes is a psychotherapist living in Nottingham, UK. He combines working with adolescents in inner-city schools with running a busy private practice for adults. James specialises in working with boys and men, and provides programmes and training to help them to increase their emotional fitness.

Renata Salecl is a philosopher and sociologist. She is Senior Researcher at the Institute of Criminology at the Faculty of Law in Ljubljana, Slovenia. She is also Professor at the School of Law, Birkbeck College, University of London and recurring Visiting Professor at Cardozo School of Law, New York. Her latest books include *On Anxiety* (Routledge, 2004) and *Tyranny of Choice* (Profile Books, 2010). Her books have been translated into ten languages.

Susie Orbach is a psychoanalyst, writer, activist and social critic. She is the UK convenor for www.endangeredbodies.org, co-founder of Psychotherapists and Counsellors for Social Responsibility, the author of 11 books and numerous articles. She has a practice seeing individuals and couples.

Dr Gail Dines is Professor of Sociology and Women's Studies at Wheelock College in Boston, USA, where she is also chair of the American Studies Department. She has been researching and writing about the porn industry for well over 20 years. Gail has written widely on pornography, media images of women and representations of race in pop culture. She is a recipient of the Myers Center Award for the Study of Human Rights in North America, and is a founding member of the activist group Stop Porn Culture. Her latest book is *Pornland: How Porn Has Hijacked Our Sexuality* (Beacon Press, 2011).

Sharon Girling OBE has been at the forefront of a national and international response to online child abuse and e-safety from which the Child Exploitation and Online Protection Centre developed; she worked at the Centre from its inception until retiring. She delivers training in the area of policing techniques and internet investigations to law enforcement practitioners and managers as well as the private sector on a national and international level. She was awarded an OBE in 2005 in recognition of her work.

Professor Liz Kelly CBE is Professor of Sexualised Violence at London Metropolitan University, where she is also Director of the Child and Woman Abuse Studies Unit (CWASU). She has been active in the field of violence against women and children for almost 30 years. She is the author of *Surviving Sexual Violence* (University of Minnesota Press, 1989), which established the concept of a 'continuum of violence', and over 70 book chapters and journal articles. In 2000 she was awarded a CBE for services combating violence against women and children.

Dr Maddy Coy is Deputy Director of the Child and Woman Abuse Studies Unit (CWASU) at London Metropolitan University and Master's course leader. She has worked in a range of specialised services for women and girls experiencing violence, and while at CWASU has completed research projects on: mapping specialised violence against women (VAW) services; men who pay for sex; a template VAW strategy; and evaluations of specialised support services. She has published book chapters and journal articles on prostitution and the sex industry, and more recently on the sexualisation of popular culture. Maddy also coordinates the CWASU's Master's in Woman and Child Abuse.

Professor Stephen D. Brookfield is Distinguished University Professor at the University of St Thomas in Minneapolis – St Paul, USA. He grew up in England and is the father of two adult children. He has written, co-authored or edited 16 books on adult learning, critical thinking, critical theory, teaching and discussion methods. He was worked with many organisations and communities to help people challenge dominant ideology, and to democratise education.

Stephen Haff is the Chief of Still Waters in a Storm, a reading and writing sanctuary in the troubled neighbourhood of Bushwick, Brooklyn. He has taught English and drama for 20 years at high schools, middle schools and colleges in Brooklyn, the Bronx, Vermont and Canada. At Bushwick High School, he co-founded Real People Theater (RPT) with his students. The company has received great acclaim in the worlds of education and theatre, and has toured North America and Europe. The *Village Voice* called RPT, 'Nothing less than a revolution'. Stephen has spoken at a number of pedagogical conferences and designed curriculum for the City University of New York's GearUp programme. He is on the faculty at the Center for Social and Emotional Education. On behalf of Still Waters in a Storm, he has opened relationships with Essex County Youth Services Commission in Newark, New Jersey, Scoil Mhuire, an elementary school in Dublin, Ireland and Mountainside Elementary School in Fort Carson, an Army base in Colorado. Stephen used to make his living writing for the *Village Voice*, *American Theater*, *BOMB* and other publications, and earned his Masters at Yale University.

Dr Adam Barnard is programme leader for Professional Doctorates in Social Practice at Nottingham Trent University, Nottingham, UK. His latest publication is Key Themes in Health and Social Care (Routledge, 2011). He has worked in higher education for over 20 years and has published articles from findings from his research in philosophy, and political and social theory.

SUBJECT INDEX

AUTHOR INDEX